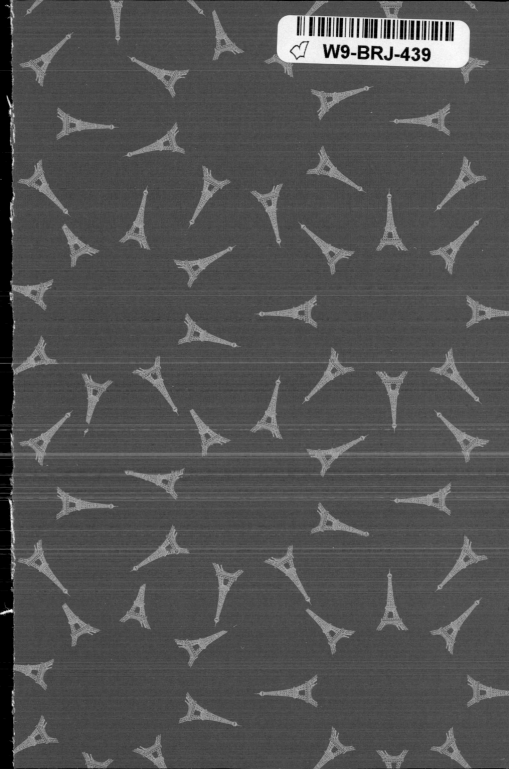
W9-BRJ-439

PRAISE FOR
JILL JONNES'S *EIFFEL'S TOWER*
(THE ADULT EDITION)

"Will transport [readers] back to a time as complex and
crazy as our own."
—*Minneapolis Star-Tribune*

"Ms. Jonnes does a fine job of walking us through the fair,
where visitors were immersed in a typical late-nineteenth-
century stew of high-minded exhibits and cheap thrills."
—RICHARD B. WOODWARD, *The New York Times*

"Exploiting the almost magnetic attraction of the great
tower, Jonnes cleverly pulls into her narrative a wide range
of characters, from 'Little Sure Shot' Annie Oakley to 'art
warrior' Paul Gauguin. . . . She does [a] . . . fine job of
demonstrating what M. Eiffel insisted all along: that his tower
was much more than just 'an object of barren wonder.'"
—ROBERT CREMINS, *Houston Chronicle*

"A colorful cast of characters descended on Paris for the
1889 World's Fair, and Jonnes (*Conquering Gotham*) offers
an atmospheric overview of the celebrities who made Belle
Époque Paris their stage during the memorable event."
—*Publishers Weekly*

"Jonnes's book is more than just a recap of perhaps the
most interesting international exposition ever staged. With
the gift of hindsight, Jonnes illuminates the roots of Belle
Époque Paris and Belle Époque Europe, a period of peace
and progress marked by technological progress and cultural
advances that lasted from the 1880s to the 1914 start of World
War I. . . . Big dreams and world's fairs benefit mankind and
make history, and Jonnes's book proves it."
—DAVID HENDRICKS, *San Antonio Express-News*

"This entertaining new work chronicles the tower's storied beginnings. . . . This carefully researched book, which combines technological and social history (and offers a lively account of the World's Fair) paints a compelling portrait of Belle Époque France."
—*France Magazine*

"In *Eiffel's Tower*, Jill Jonnes (*Empires of Light, Conquering Gotham*) presents an engaging story of a great engineer, one with an 'attractive boldness, impetuosity, and natural courage.'"
—JAMES SUMMERVILLE, *BookPage*

"In *Eiffel's Tower*, historian Jill Jonnes helps us travel back in time to the Exposition Universelle of 1889 in Paris . . . and tells the story of Gustave Eiffel's Tour en Fer de Trois Cents Mètres. Jonnes immerses us so thoroughly in the Exposition that when we get to her description of the Fair's final day, we're almost sad to leave."
—Book-of-the-Month Club

"This is a thoroughly delightful book, built around Gustave Eiffel's Tour en Fer (iron tower), but really describing in rich detail Paris and its Exposition Universelle in 1889, coincidentally the centennial of the French Revolution. Author Jill Jonnes re-creates deliciously the Belle Époque."
—JULES WAGMAN, *Milwaukee Journal Sentinel*

Eiffel's Tower

FOR YOUNG PEOPLE

Eiffel's

Tower

FOR YOUNG PEOPLE

The Story of the 1889 World's Fair

JILL
JONNES

ADAPTED BY REBECCA STEFOFF

SEVEN STORIES PRESS
New York • Oakland • London

A TRIANGLE SQUARE BOOK FOR YOUNG READERS
PUBLISHED BY SEVEN STORIES PRESS

Copyright © 2019 by Jill Jonnes
For image permissions information see page 348.

All rights reserved.
No part of this book may be reproduced,
stored in a retrieval system, or transmitted in any
form or by any means, including mechanical, electronic,
photocopying, recording, or otherwise, without the
prior written permission of the publisher

SEVEN STORIES PRESS
140 Watts Street
New York, NY 10013
www.sevenstories.com

College professors and high school and middle school teachers
may order free examination copies of Seven Stories Press titles.
To order, visit www.sevenstories.com/textbook
or send a fax on school letterhead to (212) 226-1411.

Library of Congress Cataloging-in-Publication Data

NAMES: Stefoff, Rebecca, 1951– author. |
Adaptation of (work): Jonnes, Jill, 1952- Eiffel's tower.

TITLE: Eiffel's tower for young people /
Jill Jonnes ; adapted by Rebecca Stefoff.

DESCRIPTION: New York : Triangle Square, 2019. |
Adaptation of: Eiffel's tower. New York, N.Y. : Viking, 2009. |
Includes bibliographical references and index.

IDENTIFIERS: LCCN 2018052735 (print) | LCCN 2018055091 (ebook) |
ISBN 9781609809065 (Ebook) |
ISBN 9781609809058 (hardcover : alk. paper) |
ISBN 9781609809171 (pbk. : alk. paper)

SUBJECTS: LCSH: Exposition universelle de 1889 (Paris, France)—
Juvenile literature. | Tour Eiffel (Paris, France)—Juvenile literature.
| Eiffel, Gustave, 1832-1923—Juvenile literature.

CLASSIFICATION: LCC T803.B1 (ebook) | LCC T803.B1 S74 2019 (print) |
DDC 607/.3444361—dc23

LC record available at https://lccn.loc.gov/2018052735

Book design by Stewart Cauley and Abigail Miller

Printed in the USA.

9 8 7 6 5 4 3 2 1

Contents

List of Characters

ARTHUR EDWARD, PRINCE OF WALES: (known as Bertie): heir to the throne of Great Britain; English

JAMES GORDON BENNETT JR.: newspaperman; publisher of the *New York Herald* and the European or Paris *Herald*; American, living in Paris

ROSA BONHEUR: artist; French

"MAJOR" JOHN BURKE: publicist, one of the managers of the Wild West show; American

SAMUEL CHAMBERLAIN: Bennett's editor on the Paris *Herald*; American

WILLIAM "BUFFALO BILL" CODY: owner and star of the Wild West show; hunter; former U.S. Army scout; American

NASIR AL-DIN: shah of Persia; Persian (Iranian)

THOMAS EDISON: inventor and businessman; creator of the light bulb, the phonograph, and a motion picture camera; American

GUSTAVE EIFFEL: engineer; designer and builder of the Eiffel Tower; designer of locks for the Panama Canal; French

PAUL GAUGUIN: artist; French

EDMOND DE GONCOURT: publisher and man of letters; French

GEORGE GOURAUD: business partner of Thomas Edison; American, living in England

W. FRANK HALL: Paris representative of the Otis elevator company; American

WILLIAM HAMMER: supervisor of Edison's exhibit at the Paris fair; American

GENERAL RUSH HAWKINS: U.S. commissioner of fine art for the 1889 fair; American

FERDINAND DE LESSEPS: engineer; builder of the Suez Canal; designer of the failed French attempt to build a Panama Canal; French

ÉDOUARD LOCKROY: minister of trade; commissioner of the Universal Exposition; French

ANNIE OAKLEY: sharpshooter; member of Buffalo Bill Cody's Wild West; American

WHITELAW REID: U.S. minister (ambassador) to France; American

FRANK RICHMOND: narrator of Buffalo Bill's Wild West; American

DINAH SALIFOU: king of the Nalu people of Guinea; West African

NATE SALSBURY: partner and business manager of Buffalo Bill Cody; American

ROBERT SHERARD: journalist; English

ALFRED TATE: Edison's secretary; American

THEO VAN GOGH: art dealer; brother of Vincent; Dutch, living in France

VINCENT VAN GOGH: artist; Dutch, living in France

JAMES MCNEILL WHISTLER: artist; known for the painting *Whistler's Mother*; American, living in England

CHAPTER ONE

SHOWDOWN IN PARIS

ON A JANUARY AFTERNOON IN 1888, ANNIE OAKLEY was toasting muffins and making tea in her apartment in New York City when a reporter visited. He found the place littered with guns and trophies. The famous female sharpshooter had just returned from overseas loaded with prizes, as well as valuable gifts from the continent's rich and noble folk. "I suppose a crack shot in petticoats was a novelty and curiosity to them," she told the reporter between sips of tea.

As a child in Ohio, Annie Oakley had learned to shoot by hunting game to help feed her family. Now, at the age of twenty-seven, she was famous for her performances as a star act in Buffalo Bill's Wild West, a frontier-themed open-air

The Eiffel Tower and the 1889 Paris World's Fair.

show. While performing in England with the show, she had received not just presents such as antique sugar bowls and solid-silver teapots but also, as the newspaper reported, "four offers of marriage, one from a French count." One hopeful suitor had sent her his photo along with his proposal. Oakley, who was happily married, said, "I shot a bullet through the head of the photograph, and mailed it back with 'respectfully declined' on it."

The reporter asked Oakley about her plans for the future. She said, "I will practice horseback shooting." She also hinted that she might visit Europe again, in 1889.

And she would. Soon Annie Oakley would be part of a lively crowd of French and American go-getters, artists, thinkers, politicians, and rogues drawn to the glittering European city of Paris. There the government of France was organizing the most ambitious world's fair yet. It would be called the Universal Exposition, and it would take place in 1889, one hundred years after the people of Paris launched the French Revolution by storming the prison known as the Bastille. "We will show our sons what their fathers have accomplished in the space of a century," the fair's general manager, Georges Berger, declared.

The French had held international fairs in Paris every eleven years or so since 1855. The Universal Exposition of 1889 would be more gigantic and wondrous than any before it. It was also meant to be an advertisement for the French Republic. Already the French and the Americans, citizens of two republics that were allies but also rivals, were looking to make their mark at this world's fair. Each nation was determined to uphold its honor.

Meanwhile, in France

While Annie Oakley was sipping tea and answering a reporter's questions, the people of Paris were watching the skyline of their city change. Between the familiar domes and towers, a new structure had poked up: a tower made of metal, still under construction. Its creator, a French engineer named Gustave Eiffel, was relentlessly pushing to finish the tower by May 1889 so that it would be a suitable centerpiece for the world's fair.

The remarkable structure had become a symbol of industry and modernity. It was also

NOT THE FIRST IRON TOWER

"THIS IS THE FIRST TIME ANYONE HAS DARED to propose anything of this height," wrote an admiring French engineer about Gustave Eiffel and his tower. But he was wrong.

Eiffel was not the first person to picture the sort of colossal tower that would be the centerpiece of the 1889 Universal Exposition. The original dreamer was a British railroad engineer named Richard Trevithick. In 1833 he had suggested building a one-thousand-foot tower made of cast iron in London to celebrate the passage of a major law.

From a stonework base one hundred feet wide, Trevithick's tower would narrow to ten feet wide at the top. A huge statue would stand on the summit. Trevithick died before anything could come of the project. This was a fortunate

The domes, towers, and bridges of Belle Époque Paris.

development (although not for Trevithick). Later, engineers would declare that his design was fatally flawed.

The next to propose a metal tower were two American engineers. In 1874 they offered to build a one-thousand-foot structure for the Centennial Exposition, a fair that would take place in Philadelphia in 1876 to celebrate the hundredth anniversary of the Declaration of Independence. Their design was a metal cylinder thirty feet in diameter, held in place on a stonework base by thick cables. *Scientific American* enthusiastically championed the idea, saying, "We will celebrate our centenary by the most colossal iron construction that the world has seen." This hideous chimney, like Trevithick's design, was never built.

controversial. Some people mocked the tower, some hated it, and some admired it.

Eiffel's tower was to be the tallest structure in the world, a symbol of republican France that would be visible from all directions. It would also be a blow to American pride. Just four years earlier, the Americans had finally completed their fifty-year effort to build the Washington Monument, a 555-foot (169-meter) stone pillar in the nation's capital. That pillar was the world's tallest human-made structure—but Eiffel's tower was going to be nearly twice as tall when it was completed.

Gustave Eiffel, at fifty-five, was one of France's richest self-made men. He was a successful builder of railroads and bridges. Among other engineering victories, he had solved the problem of how to design the "skeleton" inside the Statue of Liberty, and then he had built it. His company had offices in far-flung locations such as Peru, China, and Vietnam.

In the spring of 1888, Eiffel could be found on most days—sun, snow, rain, or sleet—at the Champ de Mars, a large park in Paris where the world's fairs of 1867 and 1878 had been held. Dapper in a high white collar and a top hat, he perched on a construction platform, directing his men as they put together the pieces of his colossal wrought-iron tower. His sharp blue eyes, above a dark pointed beard, missed nothing.

For nine months, Parisians had watched in fascination as the slanting legs of the structure rose. Those who hated even the idea of Eiffel's tower felt that they had been right all along. The half-built tower looked like an ugly, hulking creature.

The idea for the tower was born in 1884, when the government of France announced a contest to design and build a spectacular centerpiece for the 1889 world's fair. It was only natural that Eiffel's company would enter. Two of his young engineers and his architect created a design for a 1,000-foot (304 meter) iron tower. The idea pleased Eiffel, who made improvements to it and began promoting it as the perfect monument for the fair.

Many French were swelling with pride at the mere idea of dwarfing the gigantic American monument. An engineer friend of Eiffel's wrote in a French journal, "For a long time it seemed as if the Americans were to remain the leaders in these daring experiments that characterize the investigations of a special type of genius that enjoys pushing . . . the strength of materials to

James Gordon Bennett Jr.

their extreme limits." But now, he proclaimed, France could claim the boldest engineers: Eiffel and his firm.

But although the public did not know it, Eiffel's moment of engineering truth was drawing near. Soon he would learn if he could properly line up the four huge legs that would support the first-floor platform of his tower. Only a precisely aligned platform, perfectly flat, could safely support the rest of the immense structure.

The Wild Americans

During the summer of 1888, William F. Cody (better known as Buffalo Bill) ran his Wild West spectacle *Taming the West* twice a day on Staten Island, in New York City. The show had been a triumph across the Atlantic. In England, Queen Victoria had ordered a special command performance. Now, back on American soil, the show continued to astonish crowds with cowboys and Indians, buffalo stampedes, bronco busting, and Western whoop-'em-up. It also featured sharpshooting, but it no longer featured Annie Oakley. She was touring with a rival outfit called Pawnee Bill's Wild West.

At forty-two, Buffalo Bill Cody was famous, but as always he was also on the verge of being broke. In a letter to his sister Julia, he said, "I am tired out." But after an October rest with his family in Nebraska, he wrote to her, "Oh I am a pretty lively dead man yet—and I ain't downed by a good deal—Keep your eye on Your Big Brother." Cody was planning a new show, one that would be too fabulous for his rivals to copy. It would be an extravaganza worthy of the Paris world's fair.

Another ambitious American was already living in Paris. He was James Gordon Bennett Jr., the well-known forty-seven-year-old publisher of an immensely powerful newspaper called the *New York Herald*. It had been Bennett's idea to send the fearless Welsh journalist Henry Morton Stanley into what is now the African country of Tanzania in 1871 to search for the missionary explorer Dr. David Livingstone. Stanley found Livingstone and became the most famous journalist of his day. Bennett also introduced the idea of an interview as a news story, and early in his career he had hired talented young writers such as Mark Twain for regular columns.

Success did not protect Bennett from scandal. He had fled New York after a shocking event on New Year's Day 1877, when he drunkenly urinated into a fireplace at a party in his fiancée's home. Shunned by New York society, Bennett moved to Paris, where he lived in high style, running his newspaper by telegraph. He could have returned to New York a few years after the scandal, but he preferred to stay in Paris, where several thousand Americans were living.

Bennett had startled the French (and strengthened their view of Americans as uncouth savages) by sometimes striding into his favorite restaurants drunk and pulling tablecloths, china plates, crystal glasses, and silverware off the tables as he passed. Naked rides down one of Paris's biggest boulevards in his splendid horse-drawn coach also contributed to his reputation as a barbarian—but a wealthy one, who was welcomed by many restaurant owners for his free-spending ways.

By the summer of 1887, just as the Eiffel Tower began to take shape, Bennett had begun thinking about opening a newspaper in Paris. Late at night on the balcony of his apartment, he was mulling over the matter when he heard an owl hoot. Because he was utterly devoted to owls, Bennett took the hoot as a signal that he should go ahead with the idea. Bennett viewed owls as symbols of luck. All his estates, offices, and yachts had collections of owls made of various materials. The birds also appeared on his writing paper, coaches, and newspapers.

Within weeks of the persuasive hoot, Bennett had bought a small English-language paper that operated in Paris. He turned it into a European edition of the *Herald* and brought an experienced newspaperman named Samuel Chamberlain from New York to edit it. Bennett and Chamberlain launched themselves full force into organizing the new European *Herald*.

The timing was no accident. Bennett expected waves of Americans to descend upon Paris for the world's fair. This would guarantee the paper's success. The European *Herald* would do two things. First, it would meet the needs of Americans in Paris. Second, it would make its publisher a man of importance on two continents. Like the original *New York Herald*, the new Paris *Herald* combined high-minded political reporting with attention-getting stories about crime and high society. It also featured oddities, such as a piece about a Russian ball at which a woman died, killed by her too-tight corset.

Schemers and Dreamers

Many Americans were eyeing the Paris fair for the publicity it could bring them. One of them was Thomas Edison, an unrivaled master of self-promotion. He had invented the light bulb, and his companies had lit up cities across America. His products and inventions had been a star attraction at the Electrical Exposition, a fair held in Paris in 1881.

Now, in his huge laboratory in New Jersey, Edison was busy perfecting an improved version of the phonograph, a device for recording and playing back sound. He was about to build a new factory to manufacture the device. A *New York Times* writer who had visited the laboratory reported, "Edison's literary and musical experiments with the invention yesterday were wonderful. . . . [The machine's] possibilities are beyond calculating." Edison intended to create a big splash by making his new, improved phonograph the heart of a large and elaborate exhibit at the Paris world's fair.

Another American who intended to make a mark at the fair in Paris was the painter James McNeill Whistler. Born in Massachusetts in 1834, Whistler had lived mostly in England since

THE GOLDEN TIMES

FOR THE FRENCH AND AMERICANS, THE Universal Exposition of 1889 fell in the middle of a period that would later be recognized as a special time in the history of both France and the United States. For France, that period was La Belle Époque, meaning "the beautiful time." For the United States, it was the Gilded Age.

La Belle Époque began in 1871, just after a new government, known as the Third Republic, came into power. It was a time of growth and progress. The Paris Métro (subway), the Paris Opéra, the Eiffel Tower, and countless other structures were built or completed. World's fairs in 1878, 1889, and 1900 brought hordes of visitors to the City of Light, as Paris was called.

The arts flowered in France during La Belle Époque, especially in Paris. The first public

Paris Exposition, 1889.

screening of a motion picture took place there, and new movements in the arts were born. One of these movements was Impressionism, a school of painting that revolutionized art for painters and audiences alike. The end of La Belle Époque came in 1914, when Europe was plunged into the horrors of World War I.

Parisians who lived through La Belle Époque didn't use that term at the time. Only after World War I ended in 1918 did it come into use. *La Belle Époque* was a reminder of a peaceful, glorious time that people looked back on with nostalgia. The same thing happened in the United States, but for different reasons.

In the 1920s and '30s, people in America started using the term *Gilded Age* for the period from the 1870s to about 1900. The name came from a novel called *The Gilded Age: A Tale of Today*. Written by Mark Twain and Charles Dudley Warner and published in 1873, the novel shows a society that has serious problems but that looks "gilded" (covered with gold) on the surface.

The Gilded Age was a time when a few people (some of whom owned railroad or oil companies) built immense fortunes while vast numbers of other people, including many immigrants, lived in poverty. It was also a time when social reform movements began to gather strength as people protested against injustice and inequality. Movements to end child labor, to gain the vote for women, and to strengthen workers' rights can be traced to the Gilded Age.

the late 1850s. In early 1888 he was involved in a cultural dustup there.

The previous year, Whistler had been named president of the Royal Society of British Artists, but the club soon regretted giving him the honor. The well-known Whistler had brought new attention and status to the artists' club, but he had also banished the works of most of its members. As president, he spent the club's money to turn its gallery into a showcase for advanced or experimental modern art, works very different from those produced by most club members.

The club would kick Whistler out, but not before he said to his critics, "You elected me because I was much talked about and because you imagined I would bring notoriety to your gallery. Did you then also imagine that when I entered your building I should leave my individuality on the doormat?"

Whistler, who called himself the Butterfly, scorned the old ways of painting stuffy historical and biblical subjects. He was never happier than when scrapping with those he considered stodgy or drawing more attention to himself. Now, like every important artist, he yearned to show off his best work in Paris, where art reigned supreme and where millions of fairgoers from around the world could admire it. The fair also offered the prospect of honors and awards that could boost sales and prices.

Across the English Channel from London, a French painter would also soon be greatly interested in the coming world's fair. For now, though, his problem was money. Paul Gauguin was very much an unknown artist. Born in Paris, he had grown up in Peru, sailed the world for six years with the French Navy, and settled down in his twenties as a stockbroker in Paris, painting on the side. When the French economy weakened in 1884, Gauguin moved to his wife's home country, Denmark. He then looked for work in Panama and in the French Caribbean island colony of Martinique. He spent six months painting on the island.

In 1887 he returned to Paris broke but excited by the progress he had made in his art. He befriended the brothers Theo and Vincent van Gogh. Vincent was also a painter, and Theo was an art dealer who managed to sell several of Gauguin's paintings, although for very low prices. In February 1888, Gauguin, soon to be forty years old, wrote to Vincent, "The few works I have sold went to pay off some of my most pressing debts, and within a month I am going to find myself completely penniless . . . [M]oney questions are terrible for an artist!"

To Dazzle the World

France was counting on the coming Universal Exposition to make a statement to the world. The French hoped the fair would improve an image that had been darkened by political upheaval.

In 1852, after a period of civil unrest, France had become an empire, with Napoléon III (nephew of Napoléon Bonaparte) as its emperor. Then, in 1870, France became entangled in a losing war with the German state of Prussia. This disaster led to the fall of the empire and the founding of France's Third Republic.

During the rule of Napoléon III, France had achieved impressive things, including the modernization of Paris and the building of the Suez Canal in Egypt. But the loss to Prussia, and the political and economic turmoil that followed in France, had tarnished the country's glory.

Now the Third Republic, the new government, badly needed to show the world that France's glory had been restored. The British magazine *Engineering* noted, "Politics have done much to bring [France] into discredit among other nations; the [world's fair] will do far more to restore its prestige, and to give it even greater prominence in Art, Industry, and Science. . . . With the great mass of Frenchmen, their [fair] is the most important object within the limit of their horizon."

France had invited every nation of the world to its fair—but the great European powers responded with hostility. France's republican government might insist that the fair celebrated liberty, science, and technology. The monarchs of Europe, however, saw it as a celebration of the downfall and beheading of kings and queens.

A spokesman for Great Britain protested the very idea of a French celebration. The czar of Russia bluntly called the French Revolution "an abomination." Germany dismissed universal exhibitions as "out of date." Italy said, "The expense is greater than we could bear." Spain, Belgium, Holland, Sweden, and Romania also said no.

Only the Central and South American nations had enthusiastically accepted France's invitation.

The United States had yet to formally accept. The French republicans dismissed the royal whiners, confident that the fair would showcase France's role "as educator, benefactor, and distributor of light and bread."

With the months until opening day in May 1889 rapidly ticking by, the French commissioners of the fair and such nations as Argentina, Venezuela, and Japan had spent the previous year moving heaven and earth to complete their elaborate structures and exhibit halls.

The fair would take place on 228 acres along the Seine, the river that flows through Paris. Crowds coming from one direction would enter the fair by passing under the massive archways of the Eiffel Tower. Before them they would see, in what was now a jumble of construction, the parklike Court of Honor. Its huge fountains would pulsate with frothy sprays of water. Straight ahead would loom the gorgeous Central Dome, encrusted with tiles and statues, a gleaming burst of color to contrast with the iron tower. Behind the dome, the gigantic Gallery of Machines was rising.

France intended to dazzle the world (especially its hostile neighbors) with its own shimmering exhibition area on the Left Bank of the Seine. This area would showcase not just France's technical and industrial strengths, but also its world-famous artists and architects, its much-admired wines and foods, its history and heroes, and the exotic cultures of its colonies in Africa and Asia. A French baron was building a Cairo market street on the fairgrounds, using authentic pieces of architecture from Egypt. He was also arranging for the market to be peopled with hundreds of real Egyptians, such as goldsmiths and weavers, who would work and sell their wares in little shops.

The United States was taking its time in officially accepting France's invitation to the fair, but that did not stop American committees, companies, and artists from busily coming up with ways to outshine the French and everyone else at the fair. They were fired by national pride and the spirit of competition. The United States had become astonishingly rich since the Civil War. Its technology, industry, and agriculture were reshaping the world's economy. Its citizens felt they deserved a more prominent place on the world stage.

James Gordon Bennett Jr. certainly believed that Europe needed educating about the rising greatness of America. He planned to take on that task through his new Paris edition of the *Herald*, which would "put American ideas and American achievements on the news map of the world."

Relations between France and America had long been characterized by a mix of admiration, envy, and competition. Mark Twain had caught that spirit when he said, "France has neither winter, nor summer, nor morals. Apart from these drawbacks it is a fine country." A world's fair was just the occasion to heat up the long-standing rivalry between the world's two sister republics. On the battlefield of the fairgrounds, France and America would compete for supremacy and honors.

And so, in May 1889, accomplished and ambitious men and women of the modern world would meet on the streets of Paris. They would be players in the drama of the world's fair, acting out all the passions, rivalries, gaiety, and pleasures of Belle Époque France and Gilded Age America. This was, after all, the city that had inspired one American artist to say, "Good Americans, when they die, go to Paris." But first, they would attend the fair.

CHAPTER TWO

EIFFEL UNDER ATTACK

IN MID-MARCH 1888, GUSTAVE EIFFEL STOOD among the scaffolding of his partly built tower. What was this supremely confident engineer thinking in his chilly wrought-iron perch high above Paris? Perhaps he was simply enjoying the view that he loved and which he had described in this way:

> [T]his great city, with its innumerable monuments. Its avenues, its towers, and its domes; the Seine, which winds through it like a long ribbon of steel; farther off the green circle of hills which surround Paris; and beyond these, again, the wide horizon.

Gustave Eiffel.

Or perhaps he was in a less joyful mood. In the two years since he won the much-desired prize of building the fair's main attraction, he and his tower had endured insults, lawsuits, and political scheming. He may have been remembering that abuse.

Certainly, Eiffel was thinking about his immediate problem: how to make sure that the tower's first-floor platform was perfect. For if it failed to be level by even the tiniest amount, the tower would be thrown disastrously off vertical when it reached its full height. Then his enemies would rejoice, for what could he do then but take apart his partly built tower and admit defeat?

Endless Arguments

Eiffel had discovered what it was like to upset people. The whole world knew that his "dazzling demonstration of France's industrial power," this tower taller than any built before it, with its unique design of simple wrought iron, had stirred up endless spite and controversy.

Paris's architects had been the first to strike, and well before Eiffel's plan won the prize. They were outraged that a mere engineer and builder of railway bridges thought his iron monstrosity deserved a central place in their honored city.

In early 1885, an architect named Jules
Bourdais began promoting *his* plan as better
than Eiffel's. He wanted to build a six-story
museum of electricity, topped by a thousand-foot
stone tower called a Sun Column. The tower
would support not just a statue of "Knowledge"
but also a gigantic searchlight and mirrors to
illuminate the city. When questioned, Bourdais
would not consider any suggestion that his
design was an engineering impossibility. Not
only was it far too heavy for its foundation, but
it was unlikely to survive strong winds. Instead,
Bourdais challenged Eiffel to show how elevators
could go up and down inside *his* tower's curved
legs. Now, *that*, Bourdais claimed, was the real
impossibility!

For a year, the architects of France quietly
attacked Eiffel behind the scenes. They were
certain they could persuade the government to
choose Bourdais's Sun Column. But Édouard
Lockroy, the government's minister of trade and
the fair's commissioner, would choose the winning
design, and he clearly liked Eiffel's tower. So, in
May 1886, the editor of a French architectural
journal went noisily public. He launched the first

of many public attacks on Eiffel's tower, calling it "inartistic" and "hideously unfinished."

The very next day, Lockroy invited all who wished to compete for the great honor of building the world's fair tower to turn in their designs. Although he specified that the design should be for an iron tower, many of the 107 competitors ignored that guideline.

One of the submitted designs pictured a giant water sprinkler, in case drought struck Paris. Another suggested a tall tower built of wood and brick. Perhaps the most historically minded design was a giant guillotine, an enormous version of the device used to cut off the heads of royals and their sympathizers after the fall of the French monarchy a century earlier, during a period known as the Reign of Terror.

By now, others had joined the public campaign against Eiffel. They claimed that it was impossible for a thousand-foot tower to be safe. No building that tall could stand up to the power of the wind. They asked how Eiffel would find men willing to work at such dizzying heights. And what of the danger to visitors who went up in such a structure? One strange claim was that the huge iron tower would become a dangerous magnet, pulling the nails from surrounding buildings.

Eiffel knew that these critics were probably unaware of his vast experience. In France alone, he had built more than fifty wrought-iron bridges. He was thoroughly confident that his formula for shaping wrought iron would hold up to the worst possible winds. As for the labor question, some of his workers had already worked four hundred feet above the ground on one of his bridges. Once the tower was up, he had no doubt it would be perfectly safe. He did not bother to respond to the magnet claim.

Then came a whole new line of attack, slithering out of a poisonous undercurrent of French life. That undercurrent was anti-Semitism, prejudice against Jewish people. In June 1886, a hateful publication charged that Eiffel, through his German ancestors, was "nothing more nor less than a German Jew." An entire chapter of this work attacked the proposed Eiffel Tower as "a Jewish tower." It is sad that Eiffel even felt he had to respond. He did so in a newspaper, stating, "I am neither Jewish nor German. I was born in France in Dijon of French Catholic parents."

THE LIFE OF EIFFEL

GUSTAVE EIFFEL HAD SPENT HIS BOYHOOD
expecting to run his rich uncle's vinegar and
paint factory. But while Eiffel was finishing his
college education in Paris, his uncle quarreled
so violently with the young man's parents
that the relationship was broken. Young Eiffel
was trained in chemistry. He floundered a bit
before finding work in the growing new field of
railway engineering. Still, his employers were
so impressed with him that, at age twenty-
six, he was given a huge and complicated
project. He was assigned to build the first iron
railway bridge across the Garonne River, in
southwestern France.

Paris Exposition, 1889.

Eiffel had found his life's work. He loved designing and building huge, practical structures that conquered nature, and he enjoyed working out in the weather with his men. He was also courageous. When one of his bridge workers fell into the river, Eiffel, who was a strong swimmer, plunged right in to rescue the man. Afterward, he calmly reminded the workers, "Please be good enough to attach yourselves carefully in the future." Soon afterward, Eiffel saved yet another man and his three children from drowning when their boat turned over in a raging storm.

In 1862, Eiffel married a young woman from his hometown of Dijon. They would eventually have

five children. By 1867, with financial backing from his family, he had started his own engineering company. At once he won an important contract to build an iron-and-glass Palace of Machines for that year's Paris world's fair. After this success, Eiffel went on to design many railway bridges that were noted for their strength and elegance. In 1885 he welcomed his son-in-law, a mining engineer, into the company.

By his forties, Eiffel was gaining fame and wealth. His company was increasing its work in faraway places outside France. Just ahead, however, was a project closer to home, in the center of Paris: the tower that would make or break Eiffel's reputation.

Victory

On June 12, 1886, Eiffel was thrilled to learn that he had won the competition to build the fair's centerpiece. Commissioner Lockroy, in spite of the determined efforts of Eiffel's enemies, to no one's surprise had selected Eiffel's tower.

Lockroy had found all the other designs submitted either unworkable or, in the case of the gigantic replica of a guillotine, simply in poor taste. He praised Eiffel's design as "having a distinctive character" and called it "an original masterpiece of work in metal."

Eiffel, Lockroy believed, would build a powerful symbol of France's modern industrial might. The tower would celebrate science and industry, and it would draw millions of visitors to Paris for the fair, people who would come just so they could go up in the tallest structure in the world. The tower would also show France's superiority over rival nations, especially America. After all, British and American engineers had dreamed of building a wonderfully tall tower, but they had not been able to do so. The Frenchman Eiffel had solved the mystery and would build his tower with elegance and artistry.

During this time of attacks and controversy, an English reporter who sought out Eiffel was somewhat surprised to find that the engineer's office was located in a modest town house on a quiet street. Once inside, however, the reporter found more of what he had been expecting: a waiting room with rich furnishings, thick carpets, flowers, and potted palm trees. He wrote of "plans and designs of gigantic enterprises" hanging on the walls. Eiffel's private office was also "decorated with pictures of his triumphs over iron and steel."

Eiffel was always persuasive when he spoke about the design of his tower, its safety, and its beauty. He was, though, noticeably touchy on the subject of its practical purpose. What actual use would the tower have?

He repeatedly insisted that the Eiffel Tower would serve many important needs. It would be used in the study of scientific subjects such as weather and flight, in communications, and even in military strategy. "A program has already been drawn up by our scientific men," Eiffel declared, which would include "the study of the fall of bodies through the air" and other investigations. He said, "[T]here are few scientific men who do not hope at this moment to carry out, by the help of the tower, some experiment."

The path to the tower, however, would not be smooth. New obstacles lay ahead.

Money Troubles and More

After the joy of being chosen to build the world's fair centerpiece, Eiffel entered another painful phase. Now the problem was money.

Eiffel estimated the cost of building the tower at 5 million francs, equal to 1 million U.S. dollars. The French government had originally talked about covering the whole amount, but now it had changed its tune. It offered Eiffel 1.5 million francs, less than a third of the estimated cost. He would be responsible for raising the rest of the money.

To attract people to invest in his tower, Eiffel would be allowed to keep the tower up for twenty years. All profits from entry fees and restaurants in the tower during that period would go to him, and from this money he could repay his investors. But after Eiffel reached this agreement with the government, weeks and then months passed with no action and no contract. Eiffel began to worry about ever getting started on the project, much less finished.

Next, debates arose about where to locate the tower. Eiffel wanted it to stand on the Champ de Mars, with the rest of the fair. Some argued against that location, which was in the bottom of the Seine Valley. They thought the tower should be built on a hill, where it would stand out more. Others fretted that people would not pay to visit a monument located on some distant hill. In the end, Eiffel's plan carried the day.

Then the French military discovered that its training ground on the Champ de Mars would be given up to the Eiffel Tower—not just for the fair, but for twenty years. The military succeeded in getting the government to move the tower's location to a part of the Champ de Mars that was much closer to the river. Eiffel was working in his office when he learned that he now had to build his tower so close to the Seine that two of the foundations for the legs would require more complicated and expensive construction methods.

Eiffel grew more and more distressed by the delay in the confirmation of his contract. He could not start work without it. Finally, on October 22, the government committee met to debate the contract.

Several politicians spoke out fiercely against the tower. One called it "anti-artistic" and "contrary to French genius." He added that the project was "more in character with America (where taste is not yet very developed) than Europe, much less France."

Another did not want to build the tower, which "would be absurd, perhaps ugly," just to attract foreigners. He questioned why the French government should give Eiffel 1.5 million francs "so all of England can ascend a thousand feet above the banks of the Seine."

The tower's supporters pointed out that only one man, Gustave Eiffel, had stepped forward with a completely original monument that he would help finance and that could be built in time for the fair. But when the meeting ended, there had been no vote—and no contract.

New Attacks

Week after autumn week drifted by. Still there was no vote.

At last, on November 22, the committee met again. Certain members delivered the same angry speeches against Eiffel and the tower but, in the end, the politicians voted 21 to 11 to pay the agreed-upon sum toward the tower. Two days later, however, events took a disastrous turn.

A countess who lived near the Champ de Mars, along with one of her neighbors, filed lawsuits to block the building of the tower. The *New York Times* reported on the case: "[The countess] holds that the building of the Eiffel Tower is not only a menace to her houses, but that it will block up for many years the most agreeable part of the Champ de Mars, and the only one in which she has been accustomed to take her daily exercise."

Many of the countess's neighbors imagined the wrought-iron giant towering over them and felt equally nervous about living in its shadow. They feared it could collapse, or perhaps act as a gigantic lightning rod, attracting dangerous bolts during storms. Worst of all, this overpowering structure would not disappear when the fair ended. It would menace them for twenty years.

Eiffel's brief sense of triumph was gone. For the tower to be ready in time for the fair, he should be building it *now*.

He spent the cold and snowy December of 1886 in an agony of frustration and indecision.

He still had not even received the contract from the government, much less the government's money. Even if he could sign a contract tomorrow, the lawsuits would prevent him from starting construction.

Meanwhile, he was already spending a considerable amount of money. He was having engineering drawings made: 1,700 of them for the skeleton of the tower and 3,629 detailed images of the 18,000 wrought-iron sections. If construction did not start soon, all this time, effort, and money would be wasted. And what about the lawsuits?

Eiffel wondered whether *he* should offer to cover any damages that might come from the lawsuits or the possible collapse of his tower. Should he offer to raise privately the *entire* 5 million francs needed for construction? Near the end of the year, he wrote to Lockroy, "I should have started building months ago. . . . If this goes on, I have to give up all hope of succeeding. . . . If we don't come to a definite agreement by December 31 . . . I will find it painful but necessary to give up my responsibility and take back my proposals."

Then Eiffel changed his mind. He put the

letter in a drawer instead of mailing it. Instead, he threw all caution to the wind. He would not give his enemies the satisfaction of seeing him retreat from the field.

Eiffel decided to gamble his personal fortune for the glory of seeing his tower rise over Paris. He agreed to take on any costs that might arise from the lawsuits or the possible collapse of the tower, and he hired top lawyers. He would also raise all the necessary money beyond the 1.5 million francs from the state.

This bold stroke ended the logjam. On January 7, 1887, Eiffel and the French government signed the long-stalled contract. After the tower's first year, the City of Paris would become its owner, but Eiffel would keep all income except for 10 percent, which would be set aside for the city's poor.

"Great Excavations"

On January 28, during a winter so cold that people ice-skated on the lakes in Paris's parks, Eiffel broke ground at the Champ de Mars. At last, the foundations for the tower were begun.

Eiffel later confessed in a lecture that he felt tremendous satisfaction that morning: "I

The Eiffel Tower
foundation on
April 17, 1887.

watched an army of diggers start on those great excavations that were to hold the four feet of this Tower that had been a subject of constant concern for me for more than two years. I also felt that . . . public opinion was on my side, and that a host of unknown friends were preparing to welcome this daring attempt as it rose out of the ground."

Each of the tower's four immense feet marked a point of the compass. The east and south feet would stand firmly on packed soil with a solid foundation of chalk beneath it. The north and west feet were closer to the river. They needed more complex foundations, which had to be excavated by means of caissons. These large watertight chambers allowed laborers to work in wet earth. Although the caissons were open at the bottom, compressed air kept water from flowing in. As the work of digging went on, the caissons would sink lower and lower.

Every morning, through the snows and freezing weather of that harsh winter, great teams of laborers turned out to excavate the foundations. Blue-suited workmen tossed dirt and rocky debris into large-wheeled wooden wagons to be hauled away by horses.

Eiffel's "Odious Column"

As the tower began to look like a reality, its opponents launched last-ditch efforts to stop it. Forty-seven of France's most famous and powerful artists and thinkers signed an angry protest letter to one of the main organizers of the fair. The letter said that "even commercial America would not have [the] dizzily ridiculous tower dominating Paris like a black and gigantic factory chimney, crushing [all] beneath its barbarous mass. . . . [F]or the next twenty years we will see cast over the entire city . . . like a spot of ink, the odious shadow of the odious column of bolted metal."

Eiffel had suffered through so many attacks that this latest blast served only as a chance to strike back. Interviewed at his giant, noisy workshop, he said, "I believe that the tower will have its own beauty. The first principle of architectural beauty is that the essential lines of a construction be determined by a perfect appropriateness to its use."

As for whether the tower could represent France's achievements, Eiffel declared that there was plenty of patriotic glory in the "tallest edifice ever raised by man." His critics had said that the tower was "big enough and clumsy enough for the English or Americans, but it is not our style." But why shouldn't France show the world what it could do on a large scale? Eiffel predicted that the tower would be "the chief attraction" of the fair.

The Tower Begins to Rise

All winter, the Eiffel Tower's foundation holes grew deeper and broader. Each leg would be supported by a huge mass of stone and cement. Two enormous iron bolts (twenty-six feet long and four inches thick) were embedded in each foundation mass. These bolts anchored iron cylinders, to which each column would be bolted.

Convinced of the historic importance of his tower, Eiffel had hired a well-known photographer to document its construction starting in April 1887. The first images captured the sight of the four foundations emerging from the Champ de Mars. Other photographers were also charting the growth of the tower, as well as the construction of other world's fair buildings.

By late June, the heavy foundations for the legs of the tower were complete. They included a system of jacks that could raise or lower each pier as needed. These would be all-important because they would allow Eiffel to fine-tune the level of the first platform. If he failed to make it perfectly even, the rest of the tower would not rise straight up.

In July the wrought-iron legs began to take shape. These huge, awkward structures were designed to lean inward, but this made them look ready to topple over. Throughout the summer, gawkers gathered to stare. They saw horse-drawn carts arrive from Eiffel's workshops, carrying the carefully designed and numbered sections of the girders and trusses that would make up the tower. The making of these three-ton pieces was a complex business. Every piece had to be designed separately for its position in the changing height and angle of the tower.

Once the partly assembled iron pieces had arrived at the construction site, they were lifted by a crane and moved to workshops at the base of each giant foot. From there, construction crews hoisted the sections into place. They used winches (lifting devices made up of cables wound around rotating cylinders) to raise and lower heavy materials. Special cranes called derricks, with movable arms, could not only lift sections but also pivot to move them into position. And

The Eiffel Tower on
December 7, 1887.

so, the giant three-dimensional puzzle began to take shape. When the legs became too high to be put together with derricks and winches, Eiffel designed steam-powered movable cranes that could travel up and down the framework of the tower, raising sections to be installed.

All who visited the Champ de Mars came away dazzled. "When we approach it," one visitor wrote, "the construction becomes monumental; and when we reach the floor of the colossus, we are lost in wonder at the enormous mass of metal which has been combined with mathematical precision and forms one of the boldest works that the art of engineering ever dared to attempt."

By mid-October, the four legs of the tower had reached a height of 92 feet—halfway to the point where the first platform would be built. Eiffel built a supporting system of scaffolds and boxes of sand so that the legs would not fall over as they rose farther. Then another nervous neighbor filed suit, and the work was halted. Who was to say that this monstrous set of metal girders would not come crashing down at the first punishing wind? In fact, a French mathematics professor predicted that if the tower ever reached the height of 748 feet, it would be bound to collapse.

Eiffel was pressed for time. Once again, he agreed to accept legal liability for any such catastrophe. He also agreed to pay to take the tower apart if it proved impossible to complete it.

From One Challenge to the Next

During the icy first days of 1888, Eiffel supervised the building of another huge scaffold on the tower. It would hold in place the four legs that would join into a giant square frame: the first floor of the tower. This four-section frame, once joined together, would support iron girders and trusses that would encircle the legs like a thick metal belt. This first platform would be the all-important foundation for the rest of the tower.

Parisians were now used to seeing the tower grow taller almost daily. When work on the platform halted the rising of the legs, people assumed the worst. One newspaper headline warned, "The Tower Is Sinking." The article urged that the tower be taken apart as soon as possible.

The process of completing the first platform and making sure that it was perfectly level would

A PLEA FROM PANAMA

IN NOVEMBER 1887, GUSTAVE EIFFEL WAS surprised to hear from Ferdinand de Lesseps, another French engineer. De Lesseps had built the Suez Canal through Egypt, connecting the Mediterranean Sea to the Red Sea. Now he was president of the French company that was building a canal through Panama, in Central America, to connect the Atlantic and Pacific Oceans.

The Suez Canal had cut through a stretch of flat desert. It had been possible to build the entire canal at sea level. De Lesseps was trying to do the same thing in Panama, but there the landscape was rugged and mountainous. Eiffel had never believed that a sea-level Panama Canal was possible. The project had been plagued with setbacks, troubles, and reports that the sea-level plan was a disaster. The value of the company's

Men transporting
bananas to the city
markets in Panama.

stock was falling, a source of great concern to the
eight hundred thousand French people who had
bought shares in it.

Now de Lesseps was ready to admit that his
sea-level plan was a botch. He appealed to Eiffel
to rescue the canal. He could do this by designing
a system of locks, huge chambers that can be
filled with water to raise ships to a higher level of
the canal or drained to lower them. If a series of
locks could be built up and over the mountains
of central Panama like a giant staircase, the canal
should be possible.

"Oh, I hesitated. I hesitated a long time," Eiffel
wrote later. But in the end, he could not resist
the appeal to his engineer's pride, or the desire
to create another huge success for France. He
reluctantly agreed to take over as the general
contractor of the Panama Canal. He sent a team
to Panama to start work in January 1888.

take months. The crucial question was whether the "belt" of girders and trusses could both hold the tower's four legs together and maintain an absolutely level platform. Each of the four legs was made up of four corner columns. This meant that sixteen columns had to meet the belt at precisely the right height, and in exactly the spot where rivet holes had been made to fasten them. If not, the first platform would be fatally slanted.

By March 1888, Eiffel and his men were measuring the four legs, each of which weighed 440 tons. If one of the sixteen columns was off by even a fraction of an inch, the system of jacks that Eiffel had installed at the bases of the columns could be used to raise or lower it. On March 26, Eiffel and his engineers examined the first platform. It was absolutely and perfectly horizontal. "The sight of it alone was enough to brush aside any fears of its overturning," Eiffel later wrote.

The first platform was a success. Eiffel now faced an entirely different challenge of the utmost importance: the elevators. From the start, the tower had been meant to allow visitors to ascend. Yet elevators had been in use for little more than half a century. Designing elevators to go up and down the curved legs of the Eiffel Tower was a complex problem, full of danger and uncertainty. But if the crowds could not go safely and swiftly up the Eiffel Tower, what sort of attraction would it be?

CHAPTER THREE

TROUBLES ON THE TOWER

WAS THERE ANY PLACE SO DELIGHTFUL AS Paris in the spring? The chestnut trees were a pink froth of blooms. Fountains burbled to life. People strolled the streets. American writer Mark Twain had described French street life as "music in the air, life and action all about us."

By May 1888, some of these cheerful Parisian crowds were drifting over to the Champ de Mars, drawn by the spectacle of the Eiffel Tower being built. When the weather was good, the photographers would be out taking more pictures of the tower to document its rapid rise. A Paris-based reporter for a London paper declared that "[T]he enormous mass of iron which the constructors have already piled

The Eiffel Tower with the first platform finished.

up against the clouds is the amazement of everybody. When you stand at the base and look up to the skies through a colossal spider's web of red metal the whole thing strikes you as being one of the most daring attempts since Biblical days."

Each morning, soon after the workmen arrived, the rapid blows of the riveters could be heard. On gray or foggy days, the flames of the torches flickered red and orange in the upper reaches of the tower. Eiffel's two years of planning were now paying off. Each piece of the tower had been designed separately to fit precisely into its place, with calculations that had to be accurate to one-tenth of a millimeter (about four-one-thousandths of an inch). Two-thirds of the 2.5 million rivets in the tower had been put in place in the workshops, so the workers at the construction site had only to place the remaining third.

As soon as Eiffel had his all-important first platform balanced, he opened a canteen there to serve coffee and meals to his men and save them the time of clambering down and then up again to eat. On lovely spring days, the men had their lunch up in the open air and breezes. This system also let Eiffel make sure that no worker drank too much wine, which could make him a danger to himself and others.

As May turned to June, the weather in Paris became far hotter than usual. July brought sweltering days. Thunderstorms swept in, forcing the men working on the tower to scramble down for safety. When the threat of lightning passed, work continued until it was too dark to see. There could be no days off.

Some Parisians complained that the huge metal tower had changed the city's weather. They claimed it was responsible for the thunderstorms and the lingering heat. Newspaper publisher James Gordon Bennett Jr., who was always obsessed with the weather, agreed. His paper declared that "large quantities of heavy rain and thunderclouds gather round" the tower.

The sheer size and originality of the Eiffel Tower made it the center of attention, but work was advancing on the rest of the fair buildings, too. The 1889 Universal Exposition was to be laid out in three areas. The Eiffel Tower would dominate the first and most important area, the Champ de Mars, on the Left Bank of the Seine.

The tower would act as the grand entry arch for those coming to the fair across the Seine from the Right Bank.

The Eiffel Tower stood at one end of a large park. A Central Dome was being built at the other end. Twin buildings on the sides of the park would house exhibitions of the arts. Behind the Central Dome, workers were busy on the gigantic Gallery of Machines. Nearby were smaller South American pavilions, as well as the reproduction of an Egyptian street.

The fair's second area was a narrow strip of agricultural pavilions along the Seine. It would connect the Champ de Mars with the other large part of the fair, the Invalides. Here visitors to the fair would find more agricultural exhibits, the Ministry of War pavilion, and pavilions showcasing France's colonies. Among these were working native villages from Southeast Asia and Africa. A little train would trundle between the Champ de Mars and the Invalides, making getting around not just easier but another adventure for fairgoers.

Progress and Publicity

Gustave Eiffel was pleased with the rapid progress of his tower. On July 4, 1888, he welcomed eighty journalists to a summer banquet on the tower's first platform. The guests set off up the stairs in high spirits, pleased to be among the first to ascend the tower. Some of them carried umbrellas in case a thunderstorm appeared.

Once they reached the platform, the journalists savored the view of Paris's rooftops, wide streets, and parks spread out below them. Then they sat down to their festive lunch at long tables 230 feet up in the air. They could see and hear workmen, high above their heads, riveting together the second platform. Eiffel the proud builder rose, champagne glass in hand, to toast his tower. "The beginning was difficult," he said. "I faced the storm as best I could . . . I desired to show, in spite of my personal insignificance, that France continued to hold a foremost place in the art of iron construction." The journalists joined Eiffel's toast. After lunch, they clustered together amid the girders and posed for a photograph with their host.

Just ten days later, on July 14, the French holiday known as Bastille Day, Eiffel set off a fantastic fireworks display from the tower's second platform, which had just been completed. At a height of 387 feet, it was the tallest structure in Paris. Around and above the tower, the night sky burst into exploding lights of many brilliant colors and shapes, all streaming down from the heavens.

Winning Over the Workers

The people of Paris were well aware that Eiffel was racing to finish his tower in time for the fair. That's why they were puzzled in August 1888. As far as anyone could see, no progress was being made beyond the second platform. Rumors said that Eiffel had gone mad under the strain, or that unexpected difficulties with the project had driven him to give up on it.

In September, though, cranes and winches were set up to carry material to the heights, and the tower again rose visibly skyward. The workers' hourly pay rates also rose. But even as they began putting together the final six hundred feet of the tower, its slender top spire, they were restless and unhappy. Winter was

The Eiffel Tower on December 26, 1888.

A POET ATTACKS THE TOWER

Gustave Eiffel set out to win the goodwill of important journalists, including Albert Wolff, founder and editor of a paper called *Le Figaro*. Wolff had been a loud critic of the tower, but Eiffel had won him over—partly by inviting him to a meal atop the tower's first platform. After that, Wolff began praising the tower as "a grandiose marvel as it rises majestically in the air."

Wolff's change of heart did not stop *Le Figaro* from printing mocking attacks on the Eiffel Tower. In mid-July 1888, it published a work by a poet named François Coppée, who wrote:

I visited the enormous Eiffel Tower,
That iron mast with hard rigging.

Unfinished, confused, deformed,
The iron monstrosity is hideous up close
A giant, without beauty or style
It is really a metal idol,
Symbol of useless force
A triumph of brute reality.

    After thirty mean-spirited verses, the poem
ends with these lines:

And here is the great thought,
The real goal, the profound point:
—This ridiculous pyramid
We will go up it for a hundred cents.

coming. They remembered the previous winter's bitter cold, its fog and wind, and they did not look forward to more of the same. In addition, the shorter days meant fewer working hours, and shrinking pay.

On September 19, Eiffel's men rebelled. They knew that his deadline to finish the tower worked in their favor. They laid out their complaints and demanded a raise. Eiffel countered with a lower offer. At that, the men came down from the tower and went on strike.

Desperate to avoid any delay, Eiffel bargained with the striking workers for three days. Finally, they agreed to a compromise. They would get the raise they had asked for, but gradually, over a period of four months. Eiffel would also supply the work crews with sheepskin clothing and waterproof garments for protection against the coming winter, and with hot wine. He heaved a sigh of relief as he watched his crew return to work, their heavy sledgehammers ringing out the familiar rhythms of pounding in rivets, hour after hour. Once again, the tower began to rise, looking more graceful with each passing week.

Then, as Christmas approached and the tower

neared the halfway mark, trouble erupted again. One of the men complained that he had worked for ten hours but had been paid for only nine. A group confronted Eiffel, demanding further pay raises. They pointed out that from here on they would be working at greater heights than anyone in history.

Eiffel did not agree with their argument. "The professional risks remained the same," he said, "whether a man fell from 40 meters or 300 meters, the result was the same—certain death." More important, he worried that if he gave in, it would encourage more strikes at critical moments. He promised a bonus to every worker who stayed on the job until the tower was finished, and then he announced that anyone who was not on the job at noon the next day would be fired.

When noon came, almost all Eiffel's men were present and working. The few who had gone out on strike were fired and replaced. The work proceeded quickly, with the workmen in their sheepskins arriving in the freezing dawn, ascending the icy tower, warming up at the forges, and then putting in a long, cold day.

James McNeill Whistler.

Artists' Adventures

Eiffel and his workmen were not the only ones preparing to make a grand showing at the Universal Exposition. Artists were also maneuvering to win praise and prizes at the fair.

Back in the spring of 1888, American painter James McNeill Whistler had criticized an art collector who owned some of Whistler's works but had refused to lend one of them to a show. The painter said that he hoped the collector would not be cruel enough to hold them back from the fair in Paris.

Whistler was having an eventful year. In the early summer, he quarreled with one of his friends, the English poet Algernon Swinburne. Whistler had given a public lecture, and Swinburne had written a review of it. Whistler felt that Swinburne's review was not as worshipful as it should have been, so he sent the poet a sharply worded letter. Then, in August, he stunned the art world with a spur-of-the-moment marriage to the widow of an old friend, an architect who had recently died. "The Butterfly chained at last!" the London papers declared.

But in getting married, Whistler had broken the heart of a beautiful redhead named Maud

Franklin, who had been his model and girlfriend for fourteen years. She had even called herself Mrs. Whistler. Many of Whistler's old friends were furious at his desertion of Franklin. The artist and his new wife decided it was a good time to leave London. They went to France for their honeymoon.

That fall, the French painter Paul Gauguin made his way to the town of Arles to stay with his fellow artist Vincent van Gogh. Theo, Vincent's brother, was giving monthly allowances to both men. Theo hoped that the presence of another painter would lighten Vincent's dark moods and loneliness. Vincent had real talent, Theo believed, in spite of being unable to earn a living.

At first, Gauguin was pleased to be in Arles. He thought his fortunes had taken a turn for the better. Theo, who was an art dealer, sold a number of his paintings. But by early December, Gauguin's mood had changed. He found the landscape and the people of Arles "small and mean." He and Vincent disagreed about art and, as Gauguin wrote, no longer saw "eye to eye."

As Vincent's behavior grew stranger and even hostile, Gauguin wrote to Theo that he had decided to leave Arles and return to Paris. "Vincent and I find it absolutely impossible to live peacefully in each other's company," he said. Still, Gauguin lingered, reluctant to desert Vincent. But one night, when Gauguin walked out of the house to get some fresh air and a break from Vincent's odd behavior, Vincent followed him, waving a razor. Alarmed, Gauguin spent the night in a hotel. When he returned the next day to the house Theo had rented for the two painters, Gauguin found blood everywhere. Vincent was alive, but he had sliced off his own ear. Gauguin sent for Theo, who wondered, "Will [Vincent] remain insane?"

Vincent was taken to a hospital, and Theo and Gauguin took a train to Paris. Amazingly, Vincent seemed to make a complete recovery. In less than two weeks he was home again, and painting. Safely distant in Paris, Gauguin resumed his friendly correspondence with Vincent. He praised Vincent's recent painting of "sunflowers against a yellow background."

But Gauguin now had other matters on his mind. Like every other person in Paris, he had only to look up to see the marvel that was the almost-completed Eiffel Tower. It was a reminder that soon the world's fair would open. Gauguin had no doubt that his art must be displayed at the fair. The problem was: Where?

Buffalo Bill and Annie Oakley

Late in September 1888, Buffalo Bill's Wild West ended its profitable run on Staten Island, in New York City. The show headed south for a run in Virginia before breaking up for the season. Before all the show's Indians went home, Buffalo Bill Cody escorted seventy-five of them to Washington, DC. President Grover Cleveland hosted a special reception in the White House for Cody and some of the Indians, who wore their feathered headdresses and beaded finery.

After a financially successful season, Buffalo Bill headed by train to his house on the prairie, Scout's Rest Ranch, in North Platte, Nebraska. His beloved younger sister Julia and her husband had helped build, furnish, and run the ranch while Cody gallivanted about trying to earn one final vast fortune before retiring.

Once home in North Platte, Cody engaged in his usual squabbling with his wife. He also revealed his plan to take the Wild West show to the Paris world's fair in the upcoming year. Then he turned his attention to planning a hunt for a group of British noblemen who were visiting the ranch. With Buffalo Bill leading the way, they rode off into the southern wilderness. They intended to amble through northern Mexico before crossing the Sierra Madre range on the way to Senator William Hearst's magnificent ranch on the California coast, overlooking the Pacific Ocean.

By late 1888, meanwhile, Annie Oakley was trying her hand at a whole new theatrical venture. She was starring in a play called *Deadwood Dick: Or the Sunbeam of the Sierras.* This melodrama featured Oakley, as the Sunbeam, shooting glass balls the size of apples, filling the theater with gun smoke and leaving the audience astonished. So great were the "desperate situations" of the play that, by the end of it, twenty-five characters were dead. In later years, Oakley wrote about this play, "I never quite understood just why the press abstained from vegetable throwing but they threw not one carrot."

When not onstage, Oakley was often taking part in high-stakes shooting competitions. She clipped newspaper reports of her victories for her scrapbook. Her theatrical venture in *Deadwood*

Dick, however, proved to be short-lived. The show, never very successful, had traveled to Chambersburg, Pennsylvania. There it fell apart when the assistant manager ran off with the money. Before long, Annie Oakley, like her old employer Buffalo Bill Cody, would be thinking about Paris and the Universal Exposition.

Already the Tallest

As 1888 ended, Gustave Eiffel had two reasons to rejoice. First, he had solved the labor troubles with his workmen. Second, and far more exciting, the Eiffel Tower had become the tallest structure in the world, passing the Washington Monument in the American capital. Eiffel's pride in France showed as he crowed about his triumph over "the Americans," who had not tried to build a taller structure, "in spite of their enterprising spirit."

The Americans did not bother to hide their feelings at being surpassed. They ungraciously mocked the Eiffel Tower as "a useless structure" and compared it unfavorably with the Washington Monument, "which is, after all, more artistic than the Eiffel Tower." They claimed that the tower's great height made it appear spindly and inartistic.

In truth, the higher the Eiffel Tower rose, the more elegant it appeared. Many of its loudest early critics were won over. One of them, though, in a bout of sour grapes, wrote, "The public may go up to [the tower's] summit occasionally, but having once gazed . . . said public will go where it can find things more interesting."

But how exactly would the curious public ascend to the top of the tower? Even as Eiffel was delighting in his tower in the sky, there remained the truly serious problem of the elevators.

CHAPTER FOUR

GOING UP!

FEBRUARY 4, 1899, WAS DARK AND COLD.
A journalist who wrote under the name Hugues
Le Roux described the morning this way: "The
sky was black—the snow fell—the air was icy—
the thermometer was at two degrees below zero."
The weather was far from ideal for Le Roux, who
was scheduled to climb to the top of the nearly
complete Eiffel Tower that day. He was to be the
first journalist to ascend to such a height.

That afternoon, at the base of the tower, Le
Roux met Eiffel and some other adventurers,
including a few women. While those assembled
planned to go only to the second platform, Le
Roux would go nine hundred feet up, to where
the riveters were working. Heavily bundled

The Eiffel Tower on
February 2, 1889.

against the cold—the temperature had risen slightly to one degree below zero—the group started up the steps inside one of the pillars of the tower. The slope was easy at this point. Le Roux reported that they could chat as they climbed, and no one was out of breath when they reached the first platform.

It took a smaller party of climbers twenty minutes to reach the second platform. When this platform was completed, it would include benches so that those who walked up could rest and enjoy the views. For now, Le Roux glanced through an opening in the floor of the platform and saw "very small ducks swimming in a half-frozen pond" 377 feet below. "A shiver ran down my spine at the thought of a possible fall from this height," Le Roux later recalled. "It grew suddenly colder."

To the Iron Stairway

By the time the climbers left the second platform to go still higher, twilight was swallowing the city. "Again to the iron stairway!" Le Roux declared. At once he made an unnerving discovery. At this level, the staircase was not fastened to the tower except at the top. It swung

Artist Henri Rivière's photograph of workers up on the Eiffel Tower.

sickeningly beneath the climbers' feet. Ten had started up, but six turned back. Le Roux did not.

"Here there were neither platforms nor balconies—only the ladders poised on thick planks which rode the immensity of space!" he wrote. "The ladders were lashed together with mighty ropes! Look not to the right nor to the left! Keep your eyes only on the rung of the ladder on which you are about to place your foot!"

Le Roux felt the planks beneath his feet rocking like a ship on the ocean. He approached the edge of the third platform and looked down, straining to catch a glimpse of the base far below. "What a plunge that would be!" he wrote. "How some human creature standing here, like myself, but seized with the sudden madness that lurks about high places, might fling himself out, with a horrid shriek. . . ." Le Roux felt himself slipping and grabbed at a rope. To his horror, it was not fastened to anything. "I felt myself falling!" he wrote.

Gustave Eiffel, close at hand, said calmly, "You should never touch a rope—that one is attached only to a pulley. Had you leaned on it more heavily the consequences would not have been pleasant. . . . It is now time to descend."

The four began the half-hour descent down the tied ladders and swaying spiral staircase to the second platform. There they warmed up with hot drinks before climbing down the more secure part of the staircase to the ground.

The Missing Elevators

The journalist's climb to the near top of the Eiffel Tower had been an adventurous success. Gustave Eiffel could only be grateful that his guest hadn't asked about the elevators that were supposed to carry people up the tower. The unfortunate reality was that the tower still did not have working elevators, even though Eiffel's contract had called for them to be completed already.

In less than three months, hundreds of thousands of people would be swarming to visit the fair. Eiffel hoped that as many as a million would visit his tower over the summer. But would anyone be able to ride an elevator up it? No other problem in the construction of the Eiffel Tower had been as difficult or annoying.

Eiffel had refused to take the easy route of simply having an elevator rise straight up through the center of his masterpiece. He felt that that would destroy the tower's elegant outline. Instead, four elevators would ascend to the first platform by way of the gently curving legs. Two of these, in the north and south legs, would continue from the first to the second platform along the far more curved upper legs. And a final elevator would rise from the second platform to the pinnacle of the tower.

Early in the planning process, Eiffel and the commissioners of the fair had hired an engineer named Backmann to design the elevators. The section from the ground to the first platform was not very difficult. The tower's legs were wide enough to hold the elevators, and their curve was not very pronounced. But the section between the first and second platforms was a true problem. The legs grew narrower, and their curve in this section was the greatest of the whole tower. In an era when elevators ran not on electricity but by air or water pressure, this was a challenge like none other. And then, to reach the top of the tower, passengers would have to take yet a third elevator and rise in two stages, making a quick transfer halfway up.

Backmann chose to design only the elevator

that would run between the second platform and the top of the tower. Someone else would have to design the elevators that would run to the first platform, and from the first to the second. The goal was a swift ascent—but above all, a safe one. In addition, the fair commission had ruled that the elevators had to be manufactured by a French company. A French company was hired for the easier task—building the two elevators that would go only as high as the first platform.

But when the commission asked for bids to build elevators to the second floor, only one company responded. It was the Paris branch of Otis Brothers and Company, an American firm that had established itself as a leading elevator manufacturer, with satisfied customers around the world.

The commission rejected the Otis bid. The Eiffel Tower's elevators *must* be built by a French firm. Another call for bids went out, and again no French firms came forward. By this time, it was the summer of 1887. Eiffel was six months into the building of his tower. Work on the elevators would have to begin soon.

A Win for the Americans

With no one else willing to design and build the elevators of the Eiffel Tower, the fair commission was forced to go against its own rule and give up on the idea of French-built elevators. In July 1887, it awarded the contract for the elevators to Otis, the American company. Otis would receive $22,500 for the job of building the elevators to the second platforms. Backmann would remain responsible for the elevator from the second platform to the top.

W. Frank Hall, the Otis representative in Paris, gloried in the challenge. "Yes, this is the first elevator of its kind," he said. "Our people for thirty-eight years have been doing this work, and have constructed thousands of elevators vertically, and many on an incline, but never one [on as steep an incline as the Eiffel Tower]. It has required a great amount of preparatory study."

It soon came out that the Otis Company had been studying the matter ever since Eiffel won the contest for a tower design. "Quite so," Hall said. "[W]e knew that, although the French authorities were very reluctant to give away this piece of work, they would be bound to come to us, and so we were preparing for them."

The Otis Company, after all, had just installed the elevator in what had been the world's tallest structure up until then, the Washington Monument. The company was delighted to win the tower contract and confident that the project would go smoothly.

Little did either Hall or Eiffel dream of the dire troubles and conflicts ahead.

How Do You Stop a Falling Elevator?

Hall, the Otis representative in Paris, proposed a design of double-level elevators that would run on rail tracks. They would be moved by water power. Steam engines would pump water from the Seine up to a large reservoir on the second platform. When water from the reservoir began to flow back down, the energy of the moving water would move cylinders sunk in the ground. This would activate a system of cables and pulleys (controlled by elevator operators) that would raise and lower the elevators.

Eiffel and the fair commission felt uncomfortable with this plan. They did not like the fact that the elevators would be pulled by cables from the top, rather than pushed from the bottom, which was the European system. The Otis method seemed less safe.

Paris still shuddered at the memory of a dreadful death ten years earlier. An elevator going up in a hotel had malfunctioned and plummeted like a stone from the top floor to the basement, killing a passenger. To prevent such a disaster, Eiffel demanded "a device that permitted the car to be lowered by hand, even after failure of all the hoisting cables." Hall resisted this feature. Eiffel then insisted that the Otis Company's chief engineer, Thomas E. Brown Jr., come over from the United States to discuss the matter with him.

The Otis Company prided itself on the safety, speed, and quality of its elevators—but, above all, safety. If an Otis elevator's hoisting cables broke or stretched, powerful springs would be released. This would cause brakes to grip the rails, bringing the falling elevator to a gradual halt.

Everyone who followed the history of elevators knew of the famous moment in 1854 when Elisha G. Otis, the founder of the company, dramatically demonstrated the safety of his product by cutting the hoisting rope of a platform on which he was standing. As the platform came to a gentle stop, Otis declared to his astonished audience, "All safe, gentlemen!" But, apparently, almost forty years of proven Otis safety were not enough to reassure Eiffel and the commission.

At Odds with Otis

By the time Thomas Brown arrived in Paris in January 1888, relations between Eiffel and the Otis Company were already strained. Brown told the company in New York that it had taken him two days just to hear from Eiffel. "Meantime," Brown wrote, "we examined the Tower, and I saw at once that the bracing as constructed would not be sufficiently strong to sustain the cylinders in the position assigned to them by our plans, but I thought that a small matter of detail, which could be changed."

When Brown and Eiffel finally met, there was much discussion about how best to fit the Otis elevators to recent changes made to the tower's curved legs. There was a possibility that Eiffel would have to remove the stairways from the legs that would hold the elevators, something he preferred not to do. Brown felt that this could be worked out.

The next issue presented a far greater conflict.

Eiffel told Brown that he had not much faith in the safety of the Otis plans. For the first time, Eiffel also indicated that the fair commission, which had not yet approved the final Otis contract, would be satisfied only with the rack-and-pinion safety device that was used on many European cog railways.

For more than a quarter of a century, cog railways had been used to carry train or tram cars up and down the mountains of Europe. These devices featured a cog wheel, or pinion, that meshed with a toothed rail called a rack. The rack rail was usually set between the two running rails on which the cars traveled. As the cars rolled laboriously up and down steep slopes, the pinion moved along the rack rail, locked into position by its metal teeth. Eiffel and the commission favored this device for the tower elevators because if the hoisting cables failed, the rack and pinion would allow the car to be safely lowered to the ground by hand.

Brown was appalled. He was an expert elevator engineer. He knew that the rack-and-pinion safety device would create noise, drag, and a jarring movement as the elevators traveled up and down. He regarded the insistence on rack-and-pinion safeties as a pointless crippling of his company's machines—and said so in a twelve-page memo to his bosses in New York.

In February 1888, a top Otis executive read Brown's report. He advised Charles Otis, the president of the company, to stand firm in rejecting the rack-and-pinion device. "I should favor giving up the whole matter rather than allying ourselves with any such abortion," he wrote. "It certainly would be a serious damage to our elevator business in all Europe, and we would be the laughingstock of the world, for putting up such a contrivance."

National pride entered into the matter as well—as it did in so much of the Universal Exposition. The Otis executive pointed out that if the company agreed to design the elevators the way the fair commission wanted them, and then the elevators failed, the elevators would be "criticized by the public and the press as an American failure."

The Otis officials informed Eiffel that if he and the fair commission insisted on rack-and-pinion safeties, the company would withdraw from the contract. With no one else able or willing to build the elevators, the French were forced to back down.

Meanwhile, Eiffel had also decided once again to slightly modify the tower's legs. Of course, this meant a new round of changes to the elevator design. The Otis people later complained bitterly about Eiffel's changes. The changes rendered useless much of the work Otis had already done, and added to the engineering difficulties the elevator company had to overcome.

About this same time, Eiffel and the commission realized that they had a serious problem with a different elevator: the one from the second platform to the top of the tower. Backmann, the engineer who was supposed to design it, had turned in two designs, which included a troubling novelty: an electric motor. Eiffel and the commission rejected Backmann's plans and fired him.

With just one year until the fair opened, Eiffel now had to find a new provider for the elevator to the top. In this age before electric motors were widely accepted, the problem was the sheer distance to be ascended: 525 feet. Eiffel turned to an old classmate named Léon Édoux, an elevator inventor who had installed a very successful 230-foot elevator in a building across the Seine from the tower.

Édoux came up with a clever plan for reaching the top of the tower. The run was divided into two equal sections, and two cars were used. When one car was going up, the other came down. The weight of the descending car was used to drive water from a tank on the third platform into two cylinders, and the pressure of this water would raise the ascending car. No other weights were needed than the cars themselves.

"If There Is to Be War"

As the months ticked by in the second half of 1888, things were not going smoothly at the Eiffel Tower. Every time Eiffel made an adjustment to the inside of the tower's legs, the Otis Company had to make its own adjustment to the design of its elevators. All the extra work had forced Otis to revise the price of the two elevators upward to $30,000, an increase of 30 percent.

To make matters worse, Otis told Eiffel that because of the constant changes, the company could no longer guarantee full operation of the elevators by the contract deadline of January 1, 1889. But the elevators would be running smoothly, Otis said, by the time the fair opened on May 1.

THE NEWSPAPERMAN AT SEA

WHILE GUSTAVE EIFFEL QUARRELED WITH the Otis people about the tower's elevators, newspaper publisher James Gordon Bennett Jr. and his faithful editor Samuel Chamberlain were getting the European version of the *Herald* ready for the Universal Exposition. In the fall of 1888, with the newspaper successfully launched, Bennett set off on a cruise around the Mediterranean Sea in his luxurious yacht, the *Namouna*.

Bennett insisted that Chamberlain come along on the cruise. That way, the two men could keep close tabs on the newspaper through telegraph messages. One glorious morning after they had been at sea for several weeks, the *Namouna* approached the Greek port of Piraeus. An American navy cruiser was maneuvering between the yacht and the port. It was obvious that the

Paris Exposition, 1889.

two American vessels were on a collision course.

Bennett ordered his steersman, "Keep right ahead. That ship has no right to cross my bow." A pale-faced Chamberlain warned Bennett that hitting a U.S. warship was a bad idea. Bennett roared to his steersman not to change course. As disaster loomed, Chamberlain leaped for the helm and swung the yacht slowly around, saving Bennett from his own pigheadedness.

Far from being grateful, Bennett was furious. Within hours, he marooned Chamberlain on a desolate island (although he did leave him food and water). Only pleas and pressure from his other passengers persuaded him to send a rowboat back to fetch Chamberlain.

At the next port, Chamberlain abruptly left the yacht. His time as editor of the *Herald*'s European

Charles Otis of Otis Brothers and Company.

Eiffel was furious. In a bitter letter written on February 1, 1889, he accused Otis of not keeping its word and of placing him in "a cruel situation." He also asked why he should pay the extra charges for elevators that would be delivered so late that the tower might not be fully ready when the fair opened.

Not long after his freezing climb up the tower with journalist Hugues Le Roux, Eiffel received Charles Otis's reply. It was a long letter that admitted "the horror of the situation"—specifically, Eiffel's fear that the elevators would not be installed and ready on time. Otis regretted that Eiffel had lost confidence in the company and added that the company was "embarrassed by this state of things." But he also again reminded Eiffel that Eiffel's own continuing changes to the shape of the tower's legs were responsible for much of the delay.

Otis also defended his firm's tardiness. He said that the company's high standards were one reason that things were moving slowly. But the elevators would be working by May 1, ready for the great crowds, "unless unjust and unnecessary obstacles [are] thrown in our way by Mr. Eiffel himself."

Charles Otis also wanted Eiffel to understand that even the new, higher price did not reflect the true cost of the elevators. In fact, his company now expected to *lose* $20,000 on the contract. While Otis understood Eiffel's distress, he was angry that Eiffel had threatened to withhold payment. Otis wrote:

After all we have borne and suffered and achieved on your behalf, we regard this as a trifle too much; and we do not hesitate to declare, in the strongest terms possible in the English language, that we will not put up with it . . . and if there is to be War, under the existing circumstances, propose that at least part of it shall be fought on American ground. If Mr. Eiffel shall, on the contrary, treat us as we believe we are entitled to be treated . . . well and good; but it must be done at once, otherwise we shall ship no more work from this side, and Mr. Eiffel must charge to himself the consequences of his own acts.

Once again, Eiffel and the fair commission had little choice but to back down. The tower had to open to the public in less than six months. Eiffel had risked his own money and his reputation on making that deadline.

Return of the Sharpshooter

During that same February 1889, not far from the offices of the Otis Company in New York, Annie Oakley and her husband-manager, Frank Butler, were busy working out their own world's fair contract.

After the London run of Buffalo Bill's Wild West in 1887, Oakley had left the show with some bad feelings, though she would never explain what the problem had been. Now Nate Salsbury, Buffalo Bill's longtime partner and business manager, wanted to win her back. He used all his charm to persuade Oakley to return to Cody's Wild West show as a star attraction for the Paris run being planned.

Oakley and Salsbury had known each other since 1884, when he discovered her in Kentucky, while she was practicing for her Wild West tryout in an empty arena. He had rushed over crying, "Fine! Wonderful! Have you got some photographs with your gun?"

He hired her on the spot and paid $7,000 for the necessary publicity photos and posters.

Although she had never been farther west than Ohio, Oakley loved performing and traveling with the Wild West. "A crowned queen was never treated with more reverence than I was by those whole-souled western boys," she said. New York City was always a success for the Wild West show, and Oakley had had a few adventures there. One year, after a new snowfall, she decided to get out into the fresh air around Madison Square Garden, where the troupe performed. "I had Jerry, the big moose, hitched to a sled and thought I'd take a spin around the block," she recalled. "All went swimmingly until we turned a corner about twenty feet from the entrance and Jerry's bead-like eyes espied a push cart laden with nice juicy red apples. Three of his long strides and he was at the cart and apples flew in all directions. The vendor's hair stood on end. My moose ate the apples and my $5 paid the bill."

For Oakley, the Wild West's 1887 season in London had been one triumph after another, with gifts, compliments from royalty, and victories in sharpshooting contests. The English

Annie Oakley with her rifle.

upper crust, who prized a good shot, could not get enough of this small, quiet woman who could outshoot them all. Was it any surprise, then, that in March 1889 Oakley signed a new contract with Buffalo Bill and the Wild West? Paris and the Universal Exposition promised to be an even more wonderful, and more profitable, adventure.

Atop the Tower

While Gustave Eiffel and the Otis Company were locked in their struggle over the elevators, work on the tower itself continued at a fast pace.

The crowds on the ground could watch as a steam crane on the first platform lifted a wrought-iron section from the ground up to its level. Then the operator of a crane on the second platform lifted that same piece up to the second platform. A third steam crane working even farther up leaned down to lift up the next section of the spire.

"On the highest point reached there is a steam engine working day and night and two cranes bearing a weight of 24,000 pounds, to raise the enormous shafts of iron," a *New York Times* reporter wrote. "To get each shaft into position maneuvers lasting 20 minutes are required; the workers are placed on a movable floor rising with them and railed around, so that actual danger is reduced as far as possible." To someone looking up from the ground, the human workers were hard to see in this astonishing mechanized system.

Not surprisingly, the relentless observation of the Eiffel Tower led to rumors. In mid-January 1889, a rumor flew around that the tower had shifted and was no longer rising straight up. One publication said, "The scare in Paris this week was so great that the Exhibition authorities were obliged to send their own engineers specially to certify that everything is all right." The appearance of a shift was only an optical illusion. The tower continued to point straight up at the heavens.

Journalists clamored to see the wonders of the Eiffel Tower up close. Not long after Hugues Le Roux had climbed up the still-swaying ladders, Eiffel hosted a writer named Émile Goudeau. When he joined the riveters at the very top of the tower, Goudeau found himself almost nine hundred feet above Paris. He was wrapped in smoke from the coal-fed forges that heated the rivets and deafened by what he called "the

PROBLEMS IN PANAMA

THE ENTIRE NATION OF FRANCE RECEIVED A
SHOCK in February 1889. The Panama Canal
project was a disaster. After eight years and $300
million, a usable canal was only starting to be
built. Ferdinand de Lesseps had been desperately
trying to raise enough money to build Gustave
Eiffel's $25 million system of locks on the Panama
Canal. He had failed.

The Panama Canal Company had filed for
bankruptcy in December 1888, but de Lesseps
had immediately asked the government to let the
company reorganize and keep trying. When the
government voted down his proposal, de Lesseps
turned white and whispered, "It is impossible!

Construction of locks on Panama Canal, 1913.

It is shameful." Refusing to give up, he pressed his stockholders for more time and money. He even proposed a lottery. He launched a new canal company in January, but he sold only nine thousand out of sixty thousand shares of stock. In February the end came. The company was going to be dissolved.

Eiffel could not believe that France would let such a tremendously important project fail. He instructed his men in Panama to keep working, although at a slower pace, while they waited for the politicians to come to their senses. Meanwhile, all over France, those who had invested in the canal also clung to that hope, knowing that, otherwise, they faced financial ruin.

horrendous clangor of the sledgehammers." He wrote that the workers, "looming large against the open sky, appear to be tossing lightning bolts into the clouds."

As the tower achieved its final shape, some who had criticized it started to come around and concede to its appeal. One admirer who had received Eiffel's permission to wander about the tower's upper reaches said, "There was in this iron mountain the elements of a new beauty. . . . People admired [the tower's] combination of lightness with power, the daring centering of the great arches, and the erect curves of the principal rafters, which . . . leap toward the clouds in a single bound. . . . Lastly, the spectators were won over by what inevitably conquers everyone: a tenacious will, embodied in the success of a difficult undertaking."

There was debate over the design of the very top of the tower, which consisted of a covered gallery with a rounded roof and windows on all sides. Some thought it too complicated, that it clashed with the simple lines of the tower. Others liked it. The top could hold eight hundred visitors. Above this public gallery, Eiffel planned a series of rooms set aside for scientific purposes. There would also be a final touch that many people would envy in the coming months: an elegant personal apartment.

Above these rooms, at the true pinnacle of the tower, was the lighthouse. It was reached only by an open-air ladder. At its base was a small, narrow terrace with a metal handrail. This terrace was specially designed to hold weather-recording devices such as anemometers, instruments for measuring the speed of wind. Crowning it all would eventually be a tall flagpole.

In February 1889, an Englishman wrote a pamphlet praising and defending the Eiffel Tower. He called it "the greatest engineering work of the day" and "an object of interest throughout the entire civilized world." The writer was puzzled "why so much mud should have been thrown" at Eiffel and his tower by some parts of the press. "Why call a man mad and a fool who has sufficient pluck and ingenuity to attempt something never before attempted?" Even if the tower turned out to have no further value, the writer declared, "It will be *something* to say you have been to the top of this enormous tower."

Also puzzled by the hostility that some showed to the tower was Gaston Tissandier, a French scientist and balloonist. He said, "How many times have we not heard the remark, 'What is the use of the Eiffel Tower?' A similar question has been asked concerning almost every new thing that appears in the world."

In Tissandier's view, the tower was more than "a colossal monument for the mere attraction of public curiosity." He pointed out that it was "an experiment in iron construction of unusual importance." From it, engineers would learn many valuable lessons for future projects. Also, the tower would be part of a world's fair that fell on the hundredth anniversary of the French Revolution, the birth of modern France. "In celebrating our glorious centenary," Tissandier said, "it was desirable to astonish the world with some grand achievement the like of which had never been seen before."

In short, the Eiffel Tower was a powerful symbol of national pride and the honor of France.

Gustave Eiffel (left) poses atop his tower during the fair.

Eiffel Tower Mania

Critics found fault with the Eiffel Tower. Admirers defended it. Meanwhile, the makers of souvenirs and knickknacks were cashing in. Happily taking advantage of the world's fascination with this unique structure, they manufactured endless likenesses of it.

There were images of the tower drawn in pen, pencil, and paint. There were photographs and prints reproduced on paper, canvas, wood, ivory, china, and metal, not to mention on handkerchiefs and caps. The Eiffel Tower was eaten in chocolate and sugar candy. Cigar cases and candlesticks were made in its shape. It dangled from men's watch chains and women's earlobes. "[I]t stood in hundreds of forms in the shop-windows," said one report, "and made all idle hands busy in the workshops."

An uproar took place in February 1889. A businessman who had licensed the sole right to make reproductions of the Eiffel Tower announced that he would enforce his claim. All the businesses that would be affected threatened legal war. The Parisian peddlers who were making money by selling all the little Eiffel Towers nearly rioted. The French courts quickly ruled against the claim of sole rights. Because the state had partly paid for the tower, they said, its image belonged to the public.

With that, Eiffel Tower mania knew no bounds. Images of the tower appeared on everything from clocks to umbrella handles, from scarf pins to sleeve buttons. Eiffel Towers were made to suit all tastes and all prices. Tiny ones were sold on street corners. Elsewhere in France, small versions of the tower were built with little private dining rooms.

Gustave Eiffel was understandably thrilled. His tower was almost finished, and it was being embraced by the masses. He basked in the rising chorus of praise. Even the *Times* of London, which had been critical of the tower in its early stages, had changed its tune. "The result has not been what was predicted," it said. "Even some of those who protested most loudly against the proposal now admit that the effect of the structure is not what they anticipated. . . . [I]t has a light and graceful appearance, in spite of its gigantic size, and . . . it is an imposing monument, not unworthy of Paris."

Whatever the public thought of the tower, the owners of Paris's hotels, restaurants, and shops were waiting expectantly for the fair. They had heard that Americans would be coming in free-spending hordes, as many as half a million of them. After all, weren't all Americans like newspaper publisher James Gordon Bennett Jr.: rich and fond of spending money?

Parisian newspapers were already telling the natives how to treat the coming wave of visitors. French citizens were encouraged to conceal their natural dislike of foreigners, to treat them civilly, and to get as much money out of them as possible. "The supreme art," said one newspaper piece, "is to pluck the goose without making the creature cry out." The stage was set for an invasion of Paris by an army of American tourists.

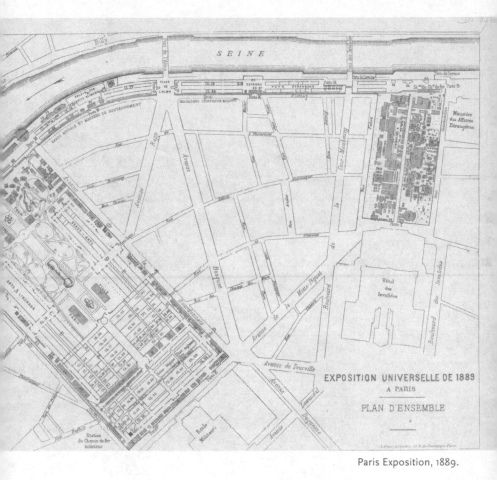

Paris Exposition, 1889.

CHAPTER FIVE

A GRAND OPENING

ON SUNDAY, MARCH 31, 1889, THE EIFFEL Tower's overall construction was completed. The pinnacle achieved a final height of 300 meters, or 984 feet. With the flagpole added, the tower reached 1,000 feet.

It had been a relentless push to get construction under way and finished on time. But, as promised, Gustave Eiffel and his men had finished in twenty-two months, in time for the fair. The day after the tower was finished, on the brisk, windy afternoon of April 1, Eiffel triumphantly welcomed guests to a ceremony at the tower. They included the prime minister of France; Eiffel's champion, the fair commissioner Lockroy; members of the press; and various

The domes, towers, and bridges of Belle Époque Paris.

high officials of the city, along with their curious wives and children.

The guests would make a formal first ascent of the tower, after which the workers would enjoy champagne. Meanwhile, not far away, laborers toiled to complete the vast, elaborate buildings, gardens, and fountains of the Universal Exposition.

Eiffel would once again lead the walk up the tower's staircase, for even the simplest of its elevators (those that would carry visitors to the first platform) were not yet ready. It was not at all clear if *any* of the elevators would be ready in time for the opening of the fair, in five weeks. But on a day of such celebration, did the absence of the elevators matter?

Pride and Patriotism

As Eiffel waited to lead his guests, a politician who suffered from dizziness used a scarf to blindfold himself, then clutched another man's arm as they started upward. The group was lively and excited. The sun came in and out of the clouds that raced across the sky. At times, the March wind gusted violently, whirling dust from below. Eiffel stopped often to explain some feature of the tower, or to let the sightseers look down at the fairgrounds or along the Seine.

When the group of one hundred climbers reached the first floor, Eiffel showed them where four restaurants would be located. There would be a French restaurant, of course. The others would be Russian, English/American, and Flemish (from Flanders, an area of northern France and Belgium). Each of the four eateries would have five or six hundred seats.

Most of the ladies in their silk spring dresses and the gentlemen in their top hats chose to go no higher. But forty of the more daring followed Eiffel up the circular staircase to the second floor. From this viewpoint, more than a third of the way to the top, these lifelong Parisians were delighted to see a new panorama of their beloved city. Below them, the Seine was a silver ribbon winding through a miniature landscape. It was an exhilarating sight, but also somehow sobering.

Half the group decided not to climb any higher. Reaching the second level had tired them, and some were beginning to feel dizzy. Only Eiffel and two dozen others stuck it out for the final half-hour climb to the top observation deck. These hardy souls included the balloonist

Tissandier, a few officials, Eiffel's son-in-law, and all the journalists.

From their lofty perch, they discovered that the city landscape and human activities were reduced to insignificance. According to the reporter for *Le Figaro*, "Paris appears like a tiny stage set. . . . The tiny black dots are the crowds. Everything everywhere looks devoid of life . . . there is no visible movement in this immensity; no noise to show the life of the people who are 'below.' One would say that a silent slumber has, in broad daylight, rendered the city inert and silent."

Up a small spiral staircase was a second glassed-in floor of four rooms. Three were devoted to scientific studies. The fourth was Eiffel's personal, well-furnished apartment. Some of the men drew back when they saw that they now had to climb yet another circular stair out into the open, where the wind was strong. Only eleven continued up. They emerged onto a tiny balcony with a slender rail balustrade (or fence). Here was the true, terrifying pinnacle of the tower.

Eiffel unfolded a gigantic blue-white-and-red French flag. As he hoisted it up the waiting flagpole, one of the journalists emotionally began singing "La Marseillaise," France's anthem since the days of the French Revolution. All soon joined in. As the flag unfurled and fluttered high above Paris, twenty-one cannon-like fireworks boomed forth from the tower's second platform.

Up on the dizzying pinnacle, the wind rushed by and the flag flapped. Eiffel's chief engineer proclaimed, "We salute the flag of 1789, which our fathers bore so proudly, which won so many victories, and which witnessed so much progress in science and humanity. We have tried to raise an adequate monument in honor of the great date of 1789." The Eiffel Tower was officially a symbol of French pride and patriotism.

The people on the pinnacle were higher than anyone had ever been in Paris, except in a balloon. They popped open champagne bottles to celebrate with toasts to Gustave Eiffel and to France. They admired the view, which was believed to reach almost fifty miles on a clear day. Then they began the long descent. Forty-five minutes later they were at the foot of the tower. Eiffel and his guests, and all 199 of his workers, sat down to lunch.

When all had eaten and drunk their fill, Eiffel

climbed up on a chair and began to speak. He declared his great satisfaction and his gratitude to all who had helped complete his tower. His remarks ended with a compliment to France—and a jab at other nations: "My goal was to demonstrate to the whole world that France is a great country, and that she is still capable of success where others have failed." The guests and workmen joined in waves of applause.

Eiffel then announced the installation of a plaque on the tower with the names of his workmen, to honor their labor. While there had been the strikes, Eiffel knew as well as anyone how hard the men had worked. Their task had forced them to deal with physical effort, terrible cold, a relentless pace, and the necessary precision and care it took to assemble a 7,300-ton structure. (Sadly, the tower had taken two lives: a worker who died in a fall, and another who was hurt in an accident and then died later from infection.)

The prime minister of France then rose to confess to admiring a tower he had originally criticized in harsh terms. To Eiffel's delighted surprise, the prime minister revealed that, in recognition of Eiffel's service to the nation, he had nominated him as officer in the National

Order of the Legion of Honor. Eiffel smiled radiantly, filled with an almost childlike happiness. His workmen presented him and his assistants with bouquets of fragrant white lilacs.

As the triumphant celebration broke up, Eiffel shook hands with his many well-wishers. It had been a great day. The Eiffel Tower, the centerpiece of the 1889 Universal Exposition, was already a great success. As Eiffel had said earlier, "The tower is now known to the whole world; it has struck the imagination of every nation, and inspired the most remote with the desire of visiting the Exhibition."

An Angry Artist

One day in late April 1889, James McNeill Whistler strolled along an avenue in Paris. The American artist looked quite dapper in his long black coat, white trousers, yellow gloves, and silk top hat, swinging a slender Japanese bamboo walking stick. His hair was tousled with its trademark white curl. At fifty-four, Whistler was still very much the witty troublemaker of the art world. He delighted in feuds. Just the previous month, he had slapped and kicked another American artist who insulted him at a London club.

On this day, Whistler's destination was the headquarters of the U.S. Commission to the Paris Universal Exposition. He was on a mission to find General Rush Hawkins, the American commissioner of fine arts. Hawkins's job in Paris was to organize an exhibit of the best art from the United States for the fair.

Hawkins felt certain that American artists had a thing or two to show the French, and a real chance at winning medals and recognition. In the area of culture, painting was America's best hope for victory. And Whistler, tiresome and eccentric though he could be, was certainly one of painting's leading figures. The meeting between him and Hawkins, however, would not be a pleasant one.

Whistler entered the mansion that housed the U.S. Commission and was directed to Hawkins's office. In his hand he held a communication from Hawkins that read, "Sir, ten of your exhibits have not received the approval of the jury. Will you kindly remove them?"

Once he was face-to-face with Hawkins, the artist said, "I am Mr. Whistler, and I believe this note is from you. I have come to remove my etchings."

"Ah," the general said, nodding, "we were very sorry not to have had space enough for all your etchings, but we are glad to have seventeen and the portrait."

"You are too kind," Whistler said, "but really, I will not trouble you."

The general slowly realized that Whistler intended to remove all his work from the fair. He would not exhibit with the other American artists. Once again, the artist's famous temper was up. Later he told a newspaper writer that he had objected to the general's discourtesy. "If the request to me had been made in proper language, and they had simply said: 'Mr. Whistler, we have not space enough for twenty-seven etchings. Will you kindly select those which you prefer, and we shall be glad to have them,' I would have given them the privilege of placing them in the American section."

Whistler gathered up his works and departed. He left behind him anger and annoyance—as he often intended. What he had not mentioned on his brief mission to stir up trouble and collect his etchings was that he intended to exhibit with the British instead, as he had been living in London for thirty years. It turned out, though, that even less space was available in the British galleries at the fair. Whistler would end up showing only a large oil portrait and two etchings.

Headaches for Hawkins

General Hawkins had other woes. As April faded into May and the opening of the fair loomed, the loss of Whistler looked like the least of his troubles.

It would be hard for anyone who had not experienced the Paris art scene to understand the complicated and important role that art played in the city. The Salon, the annual showing of French art that had been approved by a jury of art critics, was a major event. Artists competed to be included. Dignitaries such as the president of France hosted the opening ceremony. Paris fashion houses outdid themselves to have their new gowns worn by ladies at the opening. For days, even weeks, the press devoted endless columns to discussions of the painters and their work. Speculations flew about who might win a medal and launch or strengthen a career.

Artists who were rejected from the Salon called themselves the Refusés (the Rejected). To have their paintings seen, they sometimes organized their own shows. Even painters who were occasionally chosen for the Salon still decided in some years to exhibit their work with the Refusés.

As late as March, Hawkins had still been desperately trying to get an official exhibition space, some actual walls on which to hang the art chosen to represent the United States. At times, he had wondered if there would be space to display any art.

Finally, just weeks before the fair was to open, he secured two spacious rooms for the American painting exhibition. It was, in fact, the largest art exhibition space at the fair after that of the French. Now, though, he was at his wit's end trying to get the rooms ready.

The French fair commissioners insisted that Hawkins use the Parisian workmen they had assigned, and no others. Hawkins complained, "These workmen lagged and loitered and loafed and lounged in a perfectly incredible fashion." He watched with actual tears of rage in his eyes as, once again, "these white-bloused idlers" left work to get a drink.

May had arrived, and still the American exhibition rooms were not ready—nor were anyone else's. A week before the fair was to open, a reporter for the *New-York Tribune* described "the finest exhibition ever seen of packing boxes, empty showcases and machinery not in motion. No exhibition ever was ready at the appointed date. This will be the unreadiest of all, and if justice is to be done, Frenchmen will award themselves a gold medal of the highest class for unpunctuality."

A Warrior for Art

While the official in charge of organizing the exhibit of American painting struggled to get his showrooms ready in time, French artists were making their own preparations for the fair. One of the most hopeful was Paul Gauguin.

Gauguin viewed himself as nothing less than an art warrior. In his paintings he showed the modern world as it was. He fought against the kind of art that was approved by the state—the kind of work that would be shown in the fair's official French painting pavilion. There visitors would see hundreds of paintings of episodes from history and the Bible, mixed with sweet countryside scenes. Gauguin and his friends wanted to do something different, but they did not have the money to build a pavilion of their own as some of the Refusés had done in earlier years. Then one of Gauguin's friends discovered a solution.

A restaurant operator named Volpini had a contract to run a café at the fair. It would stand at the exit of the French painting pavilion. Volpini, however, was in despair. The large mirrors he had ordered to cover the walls of his café had not arrived. Gauguin's friend persuaded Volpini to cancel the mirrors, cover the walls with red cloth, and hang art on them. Gauguin and similar artists would provide the art.

Gauguin asked Theo van Gogh if his brother Vincent would like to join them. "At first," Theo later wrote Vincent, "I said you would show some things too, but they assumed an air of being such tremendous fellows that it really became a bad thing to participate. . . . It gave somewhat the impression of going to the World's Fair by the back stairs."

Back stairs or not, Gauguin was delighted with the plan. He intended to exhibit ten works, including two he had painted while living with Vincent van Gogh at Arles. He hoped that tired fairgoers who came into the café to sip coffee or enjoy a glass of wine would admire the bold modern art all around them, with its thick paint and intense colors. They might even buy a painting or two.

Vincent van Gogh, meanwhile, had had a difficult year battling his demons. He had to move from Arles because his neighbors complained that his wild behavior "frightens all the inhabitants of the quarter, and above all the women and children." By May, he was living in a mental asylum. "The fear and horror of madness that I used to have has already lessened a great deal," he wrote to Theo's wife.

A Furious Inventor

In his laboratory in New Jersey, American inventor Thomas Edison had also been preparing for the world's fair in Paris. It was the most intense period of Edison's career. As a businessman, he was overseeing the building of his various electric companies. As an inventor, he was working out the many problems of perfecting his new, improved phonograph in order to have it ready for the fair.

In June 1888, Edison had mailed a sound recording made on the new phonograph to

Colonel George Gouraud, an American who lived in London. Gouraud had befriended Edison fifteen years earlier, while the struggling inventor was visiting London on business. In the years since, Gouraud had often been a business partner of Edison's and a promoter of his inventions. In the letter he had sent with the recording, Edison explained that he would also send Gouraud "the first one of the new model [of phonograph] which has just left my hands." He added, "It has been put together very hurriedly and is not finished, as you will see."

Months later, Edison was hearing disturbing reports from London about his old friend Gouraud and the phonograph. The colonel was apparently promoting the machine as an Edison curiosity and a personal moneymaker, rather than as a serious product with great promise. One of Edison's managers told the inventor that he had heard from his father in London that Gouraud was "making a great deal of money" exhibiting the machine.

Indeed, Gouraud was besieged by crowds eager to hear the miraculous device, and he had decided to charge for the privilege. Through a long earphone, a customer could listen to several recordings. One was of remarks by Edison and the English prime minister. In another, the English poet Robert Browning read some of his own verses (with mistakes). A third recording featured Sir Arthur Sullivan, an English composer of opera music, declaring, "I am astonished . . . at the wonderful power you have developed and terrified at the thought that so much hideous and bad music may be put on record forever!"

For the most part, Edison ignored the rumors about his old friend Gouraud. He was focused on the larger issues—above all, the coming Paris world's fair. "Without doubt," he wrote to Gouraud in early March 1889, "the fair would be . . . the best opportunity, which can or will be had, to introduce the phonograph to the peoples of Europe, in fact the whole world, and as such my desire is to take every advantage of it." Edison had placed a man named William Hammer in charge of his fair exhibit, including that for the phonograph. Edison expected Gouraud to pay his share of the substantial costs of the exhibit. After all, Gouraud had been granted the copyright for the phonograph in Europe.

In late March, Gouraud confirmed the

unpleasant rumors that had reached Edison's ears. He told Edison that, yes, he had set up a phonograph in a gallery and was charging the crowds to see it. He added that the business was making him a handsome amount of money.

Edison was furious—especially when he learned that Gouraud had suggested to Hammer that they do the same thing at the Paris fair. Less than a month before the fair was to open, Edison sent a telegram to Gouraud: "Refuse absolutely to permit charging entrance fees or the introduction of any side show or Barnum methods at Paris." Edison wanted his invention to be seen as a serious, world changing piece of new technology, not as a carnival attraction.

Gouraud argued that the expenses he incurred in showing the phonograph required that he be paid for doing so. Edison then sent a telegram to Hammer: "Make no arrangement with Gouraud. . . . Intend exhibit shall be my own, at my own expense, and under my control." He told Gouraud of this decision, adding, "I will not countenance an exhibition of the phonograph for money anywhere within the City of Paris during the time that the Universal Exposition is in progress."

Perhaps Edison was quick to lose patience with his old business partner because of something that had happened earlier that year: he had learned that two of his trusted American partners in the phonograph had secretly kept a quarter of a million dollars that Edison should have received when they sold his rights to the machine. Wounded and angered by this betrayal, Edison was taking them to court.

Success and Sniping

For weeks, Gustave Eiffel had been basking in the wild success of his monumental tower. "Paris is going into raptures about the Eiffel Tower," reported the *New-York Tribune*. But while the tower might have appeared finished, it was not.

Workmen were still laboring around the clock in two twelve-hour shifts, day and night. The tower was crawling with painters. They coated the wrought-iron sections with a bronze red that lightened almost to yellow in the higher reaches. As for the elevators, the painful truth was that they were *still* not finished. All three elevator companies continued to work frantically to get their machines running smoothly.

The Otis Company, of course, was responsible

for the most difficult elevators—those between the first and second platforms. The company's representatives were irritated because French officials would not let them use American-made pumps to get the water up to the reservoir on the second platform. In addition, the reservoir was not covered, which the company thought necessary. When Otis tested its elevators, it found they did not operate as well as expected. The company insisted this failure was not its fault.

Eiffel, meanwhile, had endeared himself to every maker and seller of trinkets in Paris. Shopkeepers along every street sold Eiffel Towers in every size, "from tiny charms for watch chains to large clocks for halls." Suburban gardens sprouted Eiffel Towers complete with little flags. Even the world of fashion joined the craze. A particular shade of fabric was being called "Eiffel red."

The Americans and English continued to snipe at the French achievement. A writer for the *New York Times* described the tower as "an enormous and skillful monument of metallic construction." However, the same article said that the French considered the tower ugly. They wished that the time and money spent on it had been used for something more attractive. The writer added that the French people "are not proud to show this gigantic iron structure to strangers. . . . [T]hey vote it an abomination and eyesore."

In England, the editors of the London *Times* kept calling the tower "monstrous." One editorial in the paper did admit that the tower deserved high praise "as a mere effort of engineering." But even this lukewarm approval came with an insult to both France and the United States, for the writer pointed out that the Eiffel Tower served no purpose at all. It was only a form of showing off "more worthy of Chicago or San Francisco than of Paris."

The Fair Begins

May 6, the opening day of the Universal Exposition, dawned cool, the sky a pale blue. Two hundred thousand people jostled to attend the opening festivities. One of them was the editor of an American newspaper called the *Christian Advocate.* He wrote, "We were there early but had to struggle with the crowd for forty minutes before reaching the gate of entrance."

After a lengthy speech, the president of France led a procession through the Gallery of

Fine Arts (still not ready for visitors). There he pressed several electrical buttons. This caused the magnificent fountains in three reflecting pools at the base of the Eiffel Tower to burst into silvery life. Their waters shot skyward, then tumbled foaming down. Outside, the crowd unleashed a delighted roar and then began spreading out across 228 acres of marvels.

Not present at the opening ceremony were any British or European diplomats. The *Tribune* reported, "Such is the final response of monarchical Europe to the French Republic invitation to join in celebrating the overthrow of monarchy." The crowned heads of Europe had not forgotten that the French Revolution of a hundred years earlier had included the beheading of the king and queen of France.

The *Christian Advocate* editor stood and looked around as best he could through the happy crowd. The Eiffel Tower loomed overhead, an industrial-looking contrast to the dancing fountains and to the 195 foot high Central Dome, which was decorated in brilliant turquoise blue. The editor moved with the throngs across grounds artfully landscaped with ten thousand full-grown trees and shrubs. Thousands of

AMERICANS IN PARIS

THE UNIVERSAL EXPOSITION WAS NOT THE ONLY attraction for American tourists in Paris. There were other things to see and do. Not just the great art museum of the Louvre and the city's ancient monuments and churches, but also its cafés and gardens and, above all, its shopping.

Strangely, for decades the standard American tour of Paris had included a grisly stop at the city's morgue, conveniently located next to the famous church of Notre Dame. Mark Twain described his visit with these words:

> We stood before a grating and looked through into a room which was hung all about with the clothing of dead men; coarse blouses, water-soaked; the delicate garments of women and children; [more

Paris Exposition, 1889.

elegant items] flecked and stabbed and
stained with red; a hat that was crushed
and bloody. On a slanting stone lay a
drowned man, naked, swollen, purple.

It was also still possible, as American visitors
learned from the newspaper, to see a French
criminal beheaded by the guillotine. On May 23,
a soldier who had murdered an old woman was
executed before a small crowd of "horror seekers."
Parisian tourism had a more daring side, too.
It involved outings to places such as Le Chat Noir
(the Black Cat), a fashionable club. There actors
and singers took the stage to mock politicians,
the rich, and other members of high society, the
very audience who jammed the club.

rhododendrons were just bursting into glowing pink bloom. Colorful banners fluttered on the breeze as he walked toward the exhibition halls on paths lined with bronze and marble statues. He felt as if he were in a dreamscape from *The Arabian Nights*.

The grounds alone were amazing enough to satisfy most early visitors. Much of the actual exhibitions, though, were far from ready. One American journalist sneaked into his country's painting rooms through a boarded-up doorway. He found only half of the 341 American paintings hanging. The rest were stacked against the walls in a jumble of construction debris.

The glass-and-iron Gallery of Machines was also incomplete. Outside, it gleamed with colored glass, mosaics, and ceramic brick as though jeweled. Inside, the colossal fifteen-acre temple to engineering and industry was mostly a litter of unopened crates and half-assembled machines.

The shining exception to the tardiness in the Gallery of Machines was the Edison exhibit, which was up and running from the very first day. Hammer, Edison's Paris representative, reported to the inventor that the French president had stopped at the exhibit to hear the phonograph. Hammer also mentioned that the U.S. fair commissioners "have been more bother than assistance." They had tried to take away some space from the Edison exhibit, but Hammer reassured Edison that they had not gotten away with it.

For the editor of the *Christian Advocate*, opening day and its wonders ended with "an amazing display of fireworks." At ten o'clock at night, the Eiffel Tower was illuminated with red light and crowned with green fireworks. Thanks to Edison and the electrical lights he had invented, this was the first world's fair ever to be open at night.

The Westerners Ride into Town

For weeks before the fair opened, gigantic posters popped up all over Paris. They showed a huge charging buffalo and handsome Colonel William F. Cody, with the words *JE VIENS* ("I Am Coming"). Parisians wondered: What *are* these hairy beasts plastered on every fence? *Who* is coming? Soon the newspapers explained: Buffalo Bill's Wild West was on its way.

Buffalo Bill's show (including twenty buffalo, two hundred horses, cowboys, Indians, and

Annie Oakley) was crossing the Atlantic Ocean on a ship called the *Persian Monarch*. A few days after the opening of the Paris fair, the ship steamed into Le Havre, the main port of France. It was greeted by a tugboat full of reporters who had come from Paris in train cars rented by the show. The reporters yelled and waved at the approaching ship. Colonel Cody's answering shouts set the cowboys and Indians whooping.

Sadly, no one could leave the ship until French health authorities had examined it. That would not happen until the next day. The tugboat and its load of disappointed reporters pulled away, but they were treated to a fine banquet in Le Havre, again paid for by the Wild West show.

When the *Persian Monarch* entered the port on the following morning, the whole town turned out to see these mythic beings from America. The Wild West company manager could not believe his eyes as they docked in the harbor. "There must have been fifty thousand people there," he reported. "They were on all the docks, in the rigging of the ships nearby, even on the nearest housetops."

At last the reporters could come aboard the ship. Cody led them around, starting with the menagerie, where twenty buffalo lay calmly. "These had been the best sailors of the whole lot," Cody said. He introduced the newspapermen to the various Sioux chiefs, wrapped up in heavy blankets against the early morning chill. Meanwhile, the French health inspectors decided to give all the Indians shots against smallpox.

It had not been easy for the Wild West to bring its Indians to France. The U.S. Office of Indian Affairs (now called the Bureau of Indian Affairs) took a dim view of Wild West shows. It had only reluctantly agreed to let the Sioux go overseas. The officials of the Office of Indian Affairs thought that the Indians should be home on reservations, getting used to their new life as farmers. Cody had posted a bond of $20,000 with the U.S. government to guarantee proper treatment of the Indians in the show, and the Indians had had to get their local representative from the Office of Indian Affairs to sign off on their contracts.

Next, the French reporters met Annie Oakley. She quickly had to come up with a way to smuggle fifty pounds of gunpowder into France. French customs officers had just told her that she

could not bring in the English brand she swore by, so she poured the gunpowder into rubber hot-water bottles. When the troupe of entertainers marched off the ship, each of the show's four cowgirls had a gunpowder-filled hot-water bottle hidden under the full skirt of her dress.

The next morning in Paris, the Wild West's special train pulled into a station near Montmartre, a section of Paris that at that time was full of cottages, gardens, and windmills. Montmartre was popular with artists and writers. Here all the cowboys and Indians got off the train and led the horses and buffalo out of their railroad cars. Then the company made its way to the camp that had been arranged for it in the district of Neuilly. The cowboys and cowgirls were mounted on horses, the Indians rode in carriages, and the buffalo were led on leads.

The camp was located in the ruins of a crumbling old fort, surrounded by towering shade trees and a new, Western-style fence. Once arrived, the company pitched its two hundred tents. Horses, mules, and buffalo had their own corrals.

As the French would soon learn, the mysterious, handsome Buffalo Bill had already had a lively career. He had been a scout for the U.S. Army in the West, a rider for the short-lived

Annie Oakley.

Pony Express, and a famous buffalo hunter and wilderness guide. Now he was the star and promoter of his own show, a nostalgic celebration of the fast-vanishing American frontier.

And while Buffalo Bill had certainly been an Indian fighter in the past, he had a sympathy for the Indians that was rare in his time. He was fond of saying, "In nine times out of ten, where there is trouble between white men and Indians, it will be found that the white man is responsible." He admired the Indians' sense of honor, and he criticized Americans for failing to keep the treaties they had made with the Indians.

Cody's Wild West entertainment formula (which was imitated by many other showmen) told the story of the American West. In his version of that story, progress (in the form of white civilization) triumphed over old, backward things such as buffalo and Indians. The English had loved Cody and his show as much as the Americans. But how would the French take it? Cody was betting they would love it.

But a great deal of work had to be done before the show could open on May 18 as advertised. Among other things, grandstands had to be built to seat an audience of fifteen thousand.

The Tower Opens for Business

Nine days after the official opening of the fair,
Gustave Eiffel was at long last ready for business.
On May 15, exactly two years, four months,
and one week since Eiffel broke ground for its
foundations, the great tower welcomed its first
paying customers.

Eiffel himself was the first to sign the official
guest book. From up on the first platform
(where only one of the four restaurants was
ready to serve customers), he looked down to see
thousands lined up below. They waited patiently
to be among the first to climb up the metal
staircase—for the elevators still were not ready.
Without the elevators, no one could go all the way
to the top, the pinnacle of the whole experience.
Eiffel hoped it would be no more than another
five or six days until the elevators opened.

Meanwhile, people trooped up to the first
floor. It was decorated with the names of famous
and important Frenchmen—not rulers, but
scientists, men whose knowledge had advanced
the world. The tower was elegant, powerful,
and playful, but this message was political. In a
world where kings and queens still ruled much
of the world, the Eiffel Tower was a symbol of a

different kind of greatness. Its builder was not a king or a prince. He was a man who had made the best use of his education and his democratic opportunities to build some of the leading structures of industrial civilization.

Throughout the day, a steady line of people ascended the stairs. The hardier souls paid a second fee to press on to the second platform. There the French newspaper *Le Figaro* had opened a tiny office with a small staff and a printing press to publish a special Eiffel Tower edition. When a boy appeared with the first issue hot off the press, customers rushed for copies, knowing they would be valuable souvenirs.

Marvels of the Fair

Next to the tower, the greatest technological marvels of the Universal Exposition were found in the Edison Company's one-acre exhibit inside the Gallery of Machines. All Edison's inventions were showcased—so many, in fact, that it took *Engineering* magazine fourteen issues to cover them all.

The exhibit was a celebration of the still-new miracle of electricity. Here people had a glimpse of a future changed by technology. There were safe, easy lights for homes and workplaces. There was quick, simple communication by phone. But, of course, only the wealthy could afford such luxuries.

To Edison's delight, the unquestioned technological sensation of the fair was his newly perfected talking phonograph. The machine could certainly play music, but Edison pictured it being used "for business purposes." In Paris, the public could not get enough of it. From the opening day, many thousands of fairgoers stood in long, slow lines to hear a recorded human voice. (They could choose from among fifty languages.) The voices had been captured on wax cylinders that could be played on one of the twenty-five phonographs in the exhibit.

When someone's turn came, he nervously took the little earbuds attached by a wire to the machine, put them in his ears, and listened intently. Almost every time, a look of astonishment soon spread over his face. With so many waiting in line, each listener was limited to fifteen minutes.

Visitors who had had enough of modern machinery, or of educational exhibits about such things as making chocolate, could escape

Western civilization by drifting over to the "villages" that celebrated France's new colonies in Africa and Asia. The nearest was Cairo Street, built to reproduce an Egyptian market street. It had a crumbling mosque and whitewashed buildings set with beautiful tiles and carved wooden doors. Cheeky young donkey drivers in long blue tunics galloped up and down through the outdoor market. In the little shops of the street, Egyptian craftsmen hammered out brass trays, chiseled delicate carvings, or made leather goods, including saddles. Rug merchants served customers with glasses of tea. Cafés featured female Egyptian dancers and offered small cups of strong coffee or dishes of icy sherbet.

On Cairo Street and at the other "villages," many French citizens saw for the first time some of the peoples of their colonial empire. They could taste food from the North African countries of Morocco, Algeria, and Tunisia. They could hear the drums of West Africa, flutes from Polynesia, and gongs from Southeast Asia. They could watch the traditional dances of Cambodia and Java. The fair offered a world of new sensations, dramas, and amusements.

(top)
Javanese dancers.

(bottom)
The bustling crowds along the fair's popular rue du Caire.

CHAPTER SIX

TWO TRIUMPHS

IN THE FIRST WEEKS OF THE FAIR, BOTH
Buffalo Bill Cody and Gustave Eiffel faced
disaster—and came through to victory. Buffalo
Bill's close call unfolded on Saturday, May 18.

On that day, all of Paris seemed to stream
toward the leafy park district of Neuilly. There
the Wild West show had set up its camp and
arena, and Colonel Cody was putting on the
opening performance. The show was not open
to everyone, however. Only invited guests could
come to this grand opening.

The guests of honor were Sadi Carnot,
the president of France, and his wife. Other
distinguished guests included a former queen of
Spain, princes, counts, generals, high-ranking

Buffalo Bill
thunders into
the arena on
his horse.

politicians, and famous artists. Not a single one of the arena's fifteen thousand seats was empty. The audience was so large, in fact, that the performance was standing room only.

Most of the Americans who lived in Paris had also shown up, out of patriotic feeling for their country's production. They nervously wondered, though, what French people would think of the American spectacle, so wildly different from anything in their own culture.

Across the arena stretched a vast backdrop of painted canvas. It turned the Parisian park into the American West, with rugged Rocky Mountains dotted with lonesome pines. The show's Cowboy Band struck up a lively tune as U.S. Marines marched in. The French president and his wife were escorted to their places of honor. With that, the show began.

A Bad Beginning

Frank Richmond strode into the arena. He was the voice of the Wild West show. His speeches were a carefully crafted framework. They set the stage for the various acts and linked them together into a story.

Richmond began to deliver his narrative—not

This poster promoting the Wild West show was plastered everywhere in Paris.

in his usual words, but in a French version that he had just memorized. Up in the packed stands, the French audience furrowed its brows as it tried to figure out what language this impressive man might be speaking.

This frontier pageant, Richmond declared in the French he had learned by heart, was the real and true story of modern, nineteenth-century American progress. It told how the white man had tamed the Wild West of buffalos and Indians. He then introduced the whole company.

Scores of whooping cowboys thundered into the arena doing rope tricks. Following them more solemnly, a hundred Plains Indians presented a fearsome sight in brilliant war paint and feathered bonnets. Richmond introduced each chief by name. Next the vaqueros, or Mexican cowboys, rode past in their costumes and sombreros decked with silver ornaments. Then came the cowgirls, followed by French Canadian trappers and their Eskimo sled dogs, and of course that famous star Miss Annie Oakley.

"Last—but not by any means least," the Paris *Herald* reported, "came Buffalo Bill, who rode in like the wind on his beautifully groomed gray mustang." Almost every American in the crowd knew the details of Buffalo Bill's legendary career. But the French knew of him only from the advertising posters they had seen and a few newspaper stories. They were fascinated but somewhat mystified.

Richmond's script included helpful explanations of parts of the show, including the running of the Pony Express, the war between Indian tribes, bronco busting, sharpshooting, and the grand finale, a sneak attack on a small pioneer cabin, with Buffalo Bill himself coming to the rescue. But Richmond's French was so poorly pronounced that few in the audience knew what he was saying when he announced that they were about to see a tribe of Indians attack a group of trappers and pioneers.

Backstage, Buffalo Bill and his partner Nate Salsbury realized that something was very wrong. The audience barely responded when the Indians, vibrant with thick red, green, and blue war paint, roared into the arena, riding bareback and shrieking bloodcurdling whoops while they surrounded and attacked a wagon train. When a trumpet call signaled the arrival of the army and the defeat of the Indians, the French again showed little reaction.

The Wild West spectacle was off to a very unspectacular start.

Annie to the Rescue

Buffalo Bill turned to Annie Oakley and told her she was going on next, well before her usual place in the program. Dressed in her fringed buckskin dress, leather boots, and cowgirl hat, she entered the arena bowing, waving, and blowing kisses. Small, slender, and with nerves of steel, she coolly surveyed the grandstands. "They sat like icebergs at first," she later said. "There was no friendly welcome, just a 'you must show me' air."

She showed them.

A hollow glass ball the size of an orange whizzed through the air. Oakley whirled into action, shooting it precisely. The air was soon alive with flying objects. Oakley blasted each and every one, tossing her guns onto a table as she used up their shots. The hunters and military men in the audience could not believe what they were seeing. Finally came the long-delayed "ahs" of admiration from the crowd.

The shots came faster. Cries of "Bravo! Bravo!" rang through the smoky air. The applause built louder and louder. Oakley was shooting as fast as the wind, turning her back and whipping around to take out a number of clay pigeons. As her last hot gun hit the table, the crowd roared to its feet, throwing handkerchiefs and sunshades into the arena to show their respect.

Annie Oakley had arrived. "The icebergs were ready to fight for me during my six months in Paris," she said later.

The cheering kept up while Oakley ran to her room and made a quick costume change. Then, on her little horse Billy, she tore around the arena at full speed. With true aim, she blasted apart more glass balls and clay pigeons from horseback. Even more astounding to the audience, she shot holes straight through French coins tossed into the air. Finally, Oakley jumped off her horse and bowed. The audience stayed on its feet, cheering.

Nate Salsbury, who had discovered Annie Oakley just four years earlier, always gave her credit for saving the Paris Wild West show. Her dazzling performance won over the French, who went on to thrill to the rest of the acts: cowboys and Indians, buffalo, fights, and chases. To the relief of the nervous Americans in the audience, the

A STRANGE SNACK

EVERYTHING CONNECTED WITH BUFFALO BILL
Cody's Wild West show was a hit in Paris. Under
Cody's powerful spell, the French even snacked on
something they had never expected to eat: corn.

Corn, or maize, had its origins in the
Americas. It had been unknown in Europe until
the early sixteenth century, when Europeans
carried it across the Atlantic. Several hundred
years later, near the end of the nineteenth
century, the French still believed what they
had believed for a long time: that corn was a

Paris Exposition, 1889.

food fit only for pigs. Many Americans living in Paris had been shocked to discover that the fair featured an American Corn Palace as one of its agricultural displays. The purpose of the Corn Palace was to show Europeans how Americans used corn. The Paris *Herald* said that the success of this exhibit was "uncertain."

At the Wild West show, refreshment stands sold balls of popcorn colored pink and white. The appeal of the show was so great that French customers were willing to try these unusual treats.

Parisians decided that they loved this rollicking, romanticized version of taming the West.

The next day's newspapers made headlines of the show's triumph. "A great success in every way," the Paris *Herald* called it. Buffalo Bill Cody himself was amused to see a sudden craze for Western fashions sweep through the city. "Cowboy hats appeared everywhere on the street," he said. "Relics from the plains and mountains, bows, moccasins, and Indian baskets sold like hot cakes in the souvenir stores." The Wild West had conquered Paris.

A Huge Success

Twice each day, fifteen thousand people filled the stands at Buffalo Bill's show. Many others were turned away because the shows were sold out. One who did get in was artist Paul Gauguin. He was determined to soak up all the exotic sights of the fair, including these astonishing cowboys and Indians. Gauguin wrote to a friend, "I was at Buffalo. You absolutely have to *come see this.*" Like many other Parisians who attended the Wild West show, Gauguin bought a Stetson hat to wear.

For French citizens who wanted to better understand the mysteries of the Wild West, the

The Wild West show Indians at the camp in Neuilly, outside Paris.

show offered a fifty-page illustrated program in French. The tone of the program was serious—so serious, in fact, that much of it ended up being accidentally hilarious. Between the shameless showbiz hype and the highly exaggerated version of Colonel Cody's life, a reader might have thought that Buffalo Bill had almost single-handedly won the American West.

Before and after the show in the arena, the Parisians flocked to the Wild West's camp. They strolled along its broad gravel paths, thrilled to get a close look at a slice of the disappearing American frontier. The French were eager to see the real inhabitants of the West, a place they knew only from stories and paintings. They peered at the cowboys' large tents. They mingled with the Indian men, women, and children in their village of towering teepees decorated with painted animals. Visitors also got closer to the ponies, the twenty wooly buffalo, and the eight Eskimo sled dogs.

Annie Oakley's tent attracted crowds of admirers. Outside the tent, a cowboy raised a rope to let in visitors. Inside, a large collection of shooting prizes and trophies covered a table. At times Oakley would wear her many decorations.

"She is not even 25," one paper wrote, "and her chest is more bedecked with medals than that of an old general." In truth, Oakley would be twenty-nine that August, but in classic show-business style she had knocked a few years off her age.

The Indians Visit the Fair

About a week after the Wild West show opened, Major Burke of the show took the Indians on a special sightseeing trip into Paris and the fair. A reporter was part of the group. He wrote, "Major Burke promised his recruits to show them the big city which all good Americans hope to see before they die, and he has kept his promise."

The Indians rolled into Paris in three large carriages. Their excitement grew as they took in the ornate buildings and the wide streets filled with horse-drawn vehicles. As Major Burke led the Indians around the Universal Exposition, the fairgoers greeted them with delight.

Burke shepherded his charges through the immense Gallery of Machines, with its acres of whirring machinery and its moving sidewalks overhead. Later they returned for a close-up look at Thomas Edison's exhibits.

The Indians made their way to the phonographs. Red Shirt, one of the chieftains, listened to recorded music and speeches. The operators of the exhibit then asked him to record a message in his Sioux language for another Indian named Rocky Bear. Red Shirt's message included a war whoop. When it was Rocky Bear's turn to listen to the recording, his face showed complete surprise. At Red Shirt's shrill war cry, he dropped the earphones and said he was ready to go back to the carriages.

Accidents on the Tower

General Hawkins, the official struggling to get the American art exhibit ready, was not the only person involved in the Paris fair to have his troubles. Gustave Eiffel had problems, too.

One problem arose (or, rather, fell) on May 19, the day after the brilliant opening performance of Buffalo Bill's show. It was a pleasant May afternoon, and three of the four eateries on the first platform of the tower were abuzz with diners. Flocks of university students and young soldiers strolled about. Far below on the streets, the city's famous chestnut trees were in full, pink bloom. Far above, in the upper reaches

One view from the Eiffel Tower's first-floor promenade.

of the tower, men were still working away at unfinished details.

Suddenly, a well-dressed man on the second platform of the tower found himself coated from head to foot in yellowish paint. Shouts of surprise and dismay rose all around. More than a dozen other unlucky tourists were splattered with the same thick paint. One of Eiffel's painters up above had knocked over his bucket, creating chaos below. Seventeen victims were compensated for the damage to their ruined outfits.

The reporters at the tower office of *Le Figaro* laughed at the paint disaster. They were less amused when they later learned that, at the same time, part of a thin beam had also fallen. It had sheared off a structure near their office. "The platform was at that moment covered with people. It is astonishing that no one was hit," they said.

The next day, it happened again—not the paint, but the beam. This time a little beam fell near one of the eateries. And the day after that, a bolt hurtled through the glass ceiling of the reporters' office, piercing a seat that a man had just left. The journalists were furious. "Had he been there, he would have been killed instantly," *Le Figaro* reported. It added that a fatal accident would badly damage the success of the tower and said, "It is a miracle it hasn't happened yet."

And then it did happen. On May 24, a worker died. There is no record of exactly how he died, but his widow was paid to return to her home country of Italy. She later received a larger payment when she agreed not to take legal action in response to her husband's death.

The Moment of Truth

On top of everything else, Eiffel was still wrestling with the elevators.

Finally, on May 26, the cog railway elevators to the first platform went into operation. These made a terrible noise as they clanked up and down, but they offered a choice for people who did not want to trudge up 347 steps. The Otis elevators to the second floor, however, were still off limits to the public. (The Le Figaro staff had special permission to ride in one of them to reach their office.)

Two weeks after the tower opened to the public, a Mr. Brown of the Otis Company arrived at the fair. He had sailed from New York with one purpose: to prove to Eiffel and the

"ONLY A WALKING STICK"

A MAGAZINE, *HARPER'S WEEKLY*, REPORTED that the Americans were flocking to Paris and "as much as anybody else have helped to make the exhibition a success." On the subject of the Eiffel Tower, however, most Americans remained firmly unimpressed.

According to *Harper's*, a typical visitor met on the tower said, "Yes, fairly lofty; but lay it flat and it would not span the East River. As to height, well, take an elevator in any of the new buildings in New York, and if you want dizzy you can have quite enough of that sort of thing."

Already citizens of New York and Chicago were

Paris Exposition, 1889.

on the scene, busily competing for their cities to host the next world's fair. Some were still stung by the fact that the 1,000-foot Eiffel Tower was the world's tallest structure. They confided that they were planning a 1,500-foot tower in New York. Compared to this wonder, "the Eiffel tower would be only a walking stick." The New York tower, they said, would be topped by "the figure of an angel . . . trumpeting to the world the marvels of American industry and enterprise."

The success of the Eiffel Tower had not settled the French-American spirit of rivalry. It had only added fuel to the fire.

fair commissioners once and for all that the Otis elevators were completely safe. Only then could Eiffel open them to public use.

The test would be simple—and dramatic. The idea was to let an elevator fall and then see if the brakes worked properly and stopped it.

First, workmen filled the compartments of one of the Otis double-decker elevators with enough lead to equal a full load of people. Then they fastened ordinary thick rope to the elevator and removed the steel wire cable that usually supported it from above. Two carpenters held great hatchets, ready to cut the rope upon Brown's command.

Everyone who was there knew that if the Otis elevator plummeted to its base, it would be ruined. For a long time, anyone who wanted to reach the second platform of the Eiffel Tower would have to climb the stairs. This would greatly reduce the number of visitors who could take the third, final elevator to the top. Eiffel would suffer a serious financial loss. His reputation and that of the Otis Company would be much damaged. And critics of the tower and of France's republican government would gloat if the tower, a symbol of all that was new and modern, offered no easy way to reach its summit.

As the moment of truth loomed, Eiffel turned to Brown and asked, "Are you alarmed?"

"Only two things can happen," Brown replied. He then called out to the carpenters, "One, two, three!"

The hatchets swung, and the rope was sliced.

Everyone gasped as the fifteen-ton Otis machine began to fall. But then its movement slowed, the car swayed a bit, and then it stopped thirty feet above the ground. The thirty people present cheered madly and applauded. The Otis safety brakes had worked. Later, when Eiffel and Brown examined the elevator, they found that not a pane of glass in it was broken or even cracked.

Eiffel on Top

By the second week of June, Gustave Eiffel finally had a moment of immense satisfaction. On his tower's third floor, he watched as people stepped out of the elevator. They were the first public customers to make the complete elevator trip from the base of the tower. The Otis elevators were finally open.

The event was front-page news in Paris, although one reporter who made the journey said, "The sensation on going up can scarcely be described as pleasant, especially as from time to time the elevator gives strange little jerks." But a New York journalist was full of patriotic praise for the Otis elevators, calling them a "great triumph of American skill." Both writers spoke of the new experience of seeing Paris far below, looking like a toy town, with people as small as ants.

Other visitors had to deal with a newly discovered fear of heights. One Englishman said, "Though the hand rail is high enough, still there are thoughts of going over which are anything but pleasant. . . . It takes a few moments before one can muster nerve to walk on the edge of the platform and look over. You must have a strong head to do that."

Gustave Eiffel, too, was having a new experience. In his elegant apartment atop the tower, he lived with the weather as no one before him ever had. Dawn unfolded with superb rosy color. Thunderstorms were magnificent and terrifying, with bolts of lightning crashing all about. Nights, when the lights of Paris twinkled below like reflections of the stars, were especially enchanting. The great spotlight on top of the tower swept through the dark, illuminating

Eiffel drawn as his tower in the June 29, 1889, issue of *Punch*.

Linley Sambourne. Paris June 18. '89

whatever it passed. Far beneath, the fountains were lighted three times each evening with a rainbow of changing colors.

Before long, Eiffel was receiving all sorts of letters from the tower's admirers. Some were from women who asked flirtatiously if they could spend a night in the summit apartment. Other letters contained poems and songs inspired by the tower. One composer even wrote a symphony to the tower—not a very good one.

All parts of the tower were used. Tucked away in every available space were tiny businesses serving the visitors. Women sold cigarettes. Men sold souvenirs. One description compared the busy tower to a ship: "It was like a city hanging in the rigging of an immense steamer. The wind gusts came fresh and sharp like the sea breeze; one might take the sky, seen through the iron bars, for the perspective of the endless ocean."

Eiffel was pleased to see how people wanted to experience his tower. It made them feel part of something new, enormous, and modern. He took this as an approval of technology and progress. An air of exhilaration was created by the tower's many levels and constantly moving elevators, the excited crowds, the delicious smells wafting from the crowded restaurants, the many little souvenir and snack stands, and the busy work on the tower edition of *Le Figaro*. A lark even built its nest on the tower.

A Royal Visit

Monday, June 10, was the most crowded day of the fair. It was a holiday in England, and it seemed as if the whole country had crossed the English Channel to visit the Universal Exposition. One of the visitors was Arthur Edward, Prince of Wales, the son and heir of Queen Victoria of England.

The prince's visit greatly pleased the French. Everyone knew that Queen Victoria had called her ambassador to France out of the country just to make sure he did not attend this French celebration of the downfall of a monarchy. Yet here was her son, who had come to Paris "privately" to tour the fair that his own government had snubbed.

Perhaps Prince Bertie, as he was called, had come to see the Eiffel Tower because he understood better than his elderly mother the vital role that technology already played in modern power and national wealth. At any rate, he, his wife, and their five adult children appeared at the foot of the tower in the middle of the morning.

Gustave Eiffel, his son-in-law, and various government and fair officials greeted the royal family. (The prince spoke French well.) They then escorted the royals up to the second floor, which was mobbed with English people. With great difficulty, a path was cleared for their majesties to enter the top elevator, which had been specially furnished with benches and footstools for the occasion.

Atop the tower, officers from the British embassy in Paris waited. The prince and his family remained on the third level for barely ten minutes, just long enough to admire the view and sign Gustave Eiffel's handsome new leather-bound guest book. The royal signatures, with impressive flourishes, filled the entire first page. They were just the first of many autographs and messages that would be written in that book, mementos of the summer when the tower was new.

Safely returned to the second platform, the British royal party was steered to the office of *Le Figaro*. The prince spied the paper's guidebook to Paris and showed an interest in having one.

The Eiffel Tower, the Bolivian Pavilion (left), and the Nicaraguan Pavilion.

While the editors signed the guidebook, the prince and his group were already being swept away toward the Otis elevator that would take them down. A daring reporter tossed the gift volume to the vanishing prince. Bertie caught it, smiled, and waved jauntily as he disappeared into the elevator.

The Wild West Show

CHAPTER SEVEN

AMERICANS MEET THE WORLD

ON THE SAME DAY A BRITISH ROYAL FAMILY went up the Eiffel Tower, an American journalist named Susan Hayes Ward steered clear of the crowd around the tower. Instead, she strolled along the Seine and explored two large areas of French exhibits. They brought her face-to-face with visions of the past and showed her the wide world.

First, Ward visited the History of Habitation. This exhibit was designed to show how humans had lived from prehistoric times to the European Renaissance, which started in the fourteenth century. She bypassed the uninviting cave of very early humans. More to her taste were the reproductions of "civilized" dwellings from ancient times. She lingered in houses of the

Annie Oakley poses in a formal gown before her tent in the Neuilly camp.

Egyptians, Greeks, Persians, and Romans, which had been built as they were believed to have looked thousands of years earlier.

The exhibit also included traditional dwellings from faraway parts of the world, which seemed as exotic as those of the distant past. Ward was charmed by the picturesque houses built and lived in by such folk as Laplanders, Indians, Chinese, Japanese, Russians, Bulgarians, Central Africans, and South Americans. In many of the houses, she sampled the native cultures. Russian tea was available, or Turkish coffee in tiny cups. One house offered "baby canoes of birch bark, made and sold by Canadian Indians." "[E]ach house," she wrote, "has its own attractions."

Ward did have one complaint. Her national pride may have been slightly hurt. She pointed out that "the modern American house, with its comforts, improvements, and conveniences, has been strangely overlooked."

France's Overseas Empire Comes to Paris

Fairgoers were delighted to find so many exotic cultures so close together. One American writer could barely believe the fantastical pavilions of the South American nations. He called Argentina's pavilion "perhaps the most beautiful building on the grounds . . . [a] glittering mass of encrusted gold and flashing crystals, with color upon color like the fairy dreams of childhood."

In the Egyptian section, that same editor strolled down the Street of Cairo with its many open-air shops and coffeehouses. "There are fifty or sixty Egyptian donkeys with genuine donkey boys," he marveled. Susan Hayes Ward, who had been disappointed by the absence of a modern U.S. home at the History of Habitation exhibit, also joined the surging crowds to see the exhibits from France's new colonies in Asia, Africa, and the Pacific.

These exhibits included not just the Egyptian market street but also a Southeast Asian village that delighted painter Paul Gauguin, who wished that he could live in it. "The French colonies are bravely represented here," Ward reported, "and the French people look with intense interest on these natives of their colonies living as if at home in this great capital."

Indeed, both French and foreign visitors to the fair, once they had had enough of modern machinery and educational exhibits about chocolate making, escaped Western civilization entirely by drifting over to the "villages" showcasing France's new colonies. The Egyptian street was the nearest to the rest of the fair. It was also constantly lively, as the young donkey drivers galloped up and down through the bustling outdoor bazaar. In the street's many little shops, native craftsmen hammered out brass trays, made pottery, chiseled delicate carvings, or created leather goods, including decorated saddles. Close at hand, rug merchants served glasses of tea to their customers.

Most visitors were astonished to discover that the coffeehouses and eateries in the Egyptian section featured female Egyptian dancers. A reporter for the *New York Times* described the performance of one dancer in less-than-flattering terms, concluding with "The girls dance in bare feet outrageously painted red and yellow."

Those who tired of the delights of this little make-believe Egypt could experience France's other colonial realms over in the second section of the fair. There, as one visitor reported, "Arabs stalk majestically around in their white bournous, and permit you to inspect their tents. . . . In the Morocco pavilion dinner is being served, and two men, reclining on a carpet, dip their hands together into the dish."

In this part of the fair, many French citizens saw for the first time some of the peoples of their new, far-flung colonial empire. They were dazzled by the smells of unfamiliar foods and spices, the sounds of African and Asian musical instruments, and the sights of Southeast Asian temples and Muslim holy buildings in the North African style.

Art at Last

The American painting exhibit did not open until several weeks into the fair, and after many headaches for the man in charge, General Rush Hawkins. At the last minute, he had to battle the French fair commissioners, who had given part of the American space to other countries. As Hawkins put it, "Then the American eagle did scream and no mistake."

When Hawkins threatened to remove all the American art unless the space was returned, the commissioners gave in. Finally, the same week the Indians toured the World's Fair, Hawkins had the American painting rooms ready for viewing.

Within days, though, he had another problem

A FRENCHMAN VIEWS THE COLONIES

ONE FREQUENT VISITOR TO THE PART OF THE fair devoted to France's colonies was a viscount named Eugène-Melchior de Vogüé. He had written about the Arab countries of the Near East and had just been made a member of an elite society of scholars and learned men. De Vogüé was charmed to see the unlikely meetings that took place in this part of the fair. He mentioned "an African coastal king nibbling on Guadaloupian [sic] sweets" and a Vietnamese Buddhist "hobnobbing with a Greek priest." One night, he witnessed a happy conversation in a restaurant among French fair workers, Arabs, and black men. They chatted away as best they could.

Although he didn't know it, de Vogüé was looking at the future of Paris, a world city in which

The Decauville train pulls up near the Algerian Pavilion.

people of all races, religions, and languages—but above all from these new colonies—would settle and live. They would make the Paris of the twentieth and twenty-first centuries as international as this 1889 fair.

But while de Vogüé was touched by such surprising mingling, he was also concerned. He felt that many French people, after meeting these new brown, yellow, and black colonials, were giving in to ugly "feelings of pride and domination." The viscount saw that France was building "a colossal empire" in Africa and Asia. He felt some nervousness about how his country and its colonies would get along in the future. "All these exotic peoples, we may say, are now ours," he wrote. "[T]hey represent to us heavy obligations or great hopes."

on his hands. The American artists were complaining and squabbling among themselves. On one side were American painters who lived in Paris and had helped plan the fair, serving on various committees. On the other side were American painters who did not live in Paris but who had sent or brought their work to the fair. The first group, those who had served on the committees, had claimed the best places for themselves. They displayed more paintings, and larger ones, crowding out the other artists. "The Parisianized Americans wanted all or nearly all the available space," said one journalist who reported on the clash of the painters.

The quarrels of the American artists became a regular and entertaining feature of the Paris *Herald*. Letters to the editor were published, and in those letters the unhappy American painters unleashed their attacks. One of them wrote that General Hawkins "knows very little, if anything, about ancient or modern art, and how he ever secured the position he now holds is a political mystery. . . ." The writer said that never before in the history of Americans in other countries had there been "such injustice, unkindness, unfairness and unmanliness."

Embarrassment

No one would deny that the 1889 Universal Exposition was a 228-acre wonder. It had the tallest tower, the newest electrical devices, and many other symbols of modern human achievement, along with art, entertainment, food from around the world, and exotic colonial pavilions. But for Americans, one part of the fair fell seriously short.

The official American Exhibition was judged by the country's own citizens to be paltry and underwhelming. The tardy paintings and quarrelsome artists were not the only problem. Exhibits of commercial glassmaking, pottery, and jewelry did not impress. The American railway exhibit was compared to a train wreck. Smart, worldly Americans cringed with embarrassment at the American Corn Palace. They also cringed at an American company's life-size sculpture of the ancient goddess of love—made out of chocolate. A French critic scoffed, "Only a Yankee could have conceived the idea of creating an edible Venus de Milo."

The Paris *Herald* mournfully summed up the situation for its fellow Americans: "Our Inventive Genius Is Unsurpassable, but Our

Ignorance of the Beautiful Is Unpardonable." However, for Americans distressed by their nation's dismal showing at the fair, there were two bright spots.

One was Thomas Edison's magnificent display of inventions, with the talking phonograph as its crown jewel. The Edison display was not only a marvel of modern technology. At nine thousand square feet, it was also the largest American exhibit. As one of Edison's managers said, "It is American! It is not a commercial display, but a scientific one."

The other bright spot was Buffalo Bill's Wild West show, a living spectacle that drew thirty thousand excited audience members every day. In comparison, tens of thousands came every day to hear Edison's phonograph, while the Eiffel Tower, with all elevators working, drew about twelve thousand visitors each day.

Edison's Suspicions

Following the smashing success of his phonograph at the fair, Thomas Edison was eager to start selling the device in Europe. The rights to do so belonged to his partner Gouraud—the same partner who had angered

Edison by charging the public admission to see the phonograph in London.

The two partners had patched things up after their dispute. Now Edison began pressing Gouraud. How many phonographs could Edison ship to London, and when? On June 1, Edison wrote to Gouraud, "Phonographs are ready when you want them."

Gouraud sang the praises of Edison's machine. But he kept coming up with all sorts of reasons that it would be smart to wait for a more perfect version before plunging into sales. A decade earlier, Gouraud had successfully promoted the Edison telephone. Now he no longer seemed to be an enthusiastic go-getter.

Edison became suspicious of his London partner. He sent twenty-six-year-old Alfred Tate, his private secretary, to investigate. Tate, who found Gouraud to be a "tall, handsome man" with a "distinguished presence," made many visits to Edison House, the company's London business headquarters, to talk to Gouraud. He wanted to find out just when and how Gouraud planned to form a Continental Phonograph Company to sell Edison's machines in Europe.

Tate wrote of a day when he was finishing up a

meeting with Gouraud. An assistant came in to say that a visitor had arrived to see Gouraud. At once Tate rose to leave.

"No! No! My dear chap!" Gouraud said, putting out a hand to stop him. "Don't go yet! I make it a rule never to see any caller under fifteen minutes. It impresses them."

It did not impress Tate.

After hearing Gouraud's plans for the phonograph company, plans that were complicated and vague, Tate finally concluded, "He does not intend to invest a dollar in the business personally and for the very good reason that he has not got a dollar to invest."

Two Stars of Paris

Annie Oakley and Buffalo Bill captured the attention and imagination of the French. They were amazed above all by Oakley, especially her shooting skills while galloping on horseback. A Parisian reporter who had been dazzled by her performance sought her out in her tent. There he was charmed by her simple friendliness.

"Go see her," he wrote, "and she will give you her photograph. She even writes a few words . . . and because there's no furniture yet in her tent

Buffalo Bill in a studio portrait taken in Paris during the 1889 fair.

Eug. Pirou

23, Rue Royale
PARIS

she graciously kneels, makes two neat lines with her pencil and signs on them *Compliments of Annie Oakley*, and then stands up and hands you her picture."

Oakley loved her life with the Wild West show. She and her husband did not usually sleep in their luxurious tent, but they spent many restful hours there, sometimes napping in a hammock. She later recalled that it had been easy to have a bath in the tent, which was furnished with plenty of hot water, a collapsible bathtub, and towels. "I often took a morning dip like a wild bird," she said, "my tub on the green grass in one corner of the tent."

What did they eat? "Everything in sight!" Oakley said. "Good coffee, bread, butter, preserves, fine steaks broiled over wood coals, with fruits and berries in season."

She was proud of her skills and her toughness, too: "I could rope and hold the strongest horse. I could smile at the torrents of rain, that drenched me to the—the—well, never mind!"

In the early weeks in Paris, Colonel Buffalo Bill Cody also held court in his huge tent at the show's campground. The flap that served as the tent's front door was crowned with a shaggy buffalo head and draped with American flags. Visitors lucky enough to be invited inside found a room for receiving guests, a dining room, and a bedroom. Souvenirs of Cody's life in the wild American West were on display.

One of the guests was an American reporter for the *Herald*. He was proud to see the stream of French generals and high officials who came to pay their respects to Cody. Buffalo Bill, the reporter noted, "had an appropriate greeting for everybody."

Given his friendly nature, it was not surprising that Buffalo Bill was more than happy to join the social whirl in Paris. He had one triumph after another. Unlike many Americans in Paris, Buffalo Bill was proud of his young, rambunctious nation. He did not embarrass himself by trying to copy French styles and manners. As a result, both the Americans and the French liked him.

For some time there had been a strict "pecking order" among the Americans in Paris. Those who had lived in Paris for a long time tended to look down on mere tourists. The long-time residents snobbishly complained about the tourists' ignorance and rudeness. These complaints had existed long before the fair.

In 1878, a magazine called *The Nation* published an article on "The American Colony in Paris." It said that an American who had spent considerable time in Paris might describe a tourist this way: "The American traveller . . . does not know his place. . . . In his ignorance of custom and etiquette he will thrust himself even upon royalty. . . . [A]t the cafes you cannot get pork and beans or fried ham."

Buffalo Bill did away with such complaints because, unlike most Americans in Europe, he was completely at ease. Paris recognized him as something rare: a common man with natural nobility of character. Annie Oakley knew that that character was genuine. She said:

> *During our travels I have had opportunity of seeing [Cody's] sterling qualities put to every test. Fearlessness and independence were not a pose with him. I never saw him in any situation that changed his natural attitude a [bit]. . . . Dinner at camp was the same informal hearty humorous story telling affair when we were alone, and when the Duchess of Holstein came visiting in all her glory. He was probably the guest*

of more people in diverse circumstances
than any man alive. But teepee and palace
were all the same to him. And so were their
inhabitants.

Cody became something of an American
goodwill ambassador among the French, raising
their opinion of his country and its people. He
rented a "luxurious" apartment and entertained
there. He bought paintings and was seen to have
a good appreciation of art. He also received many
marriage proposals—fourteen in one week. It
was not always known that he had a wife back in
Nebraska.

One journalist wrote that all Americans
basked in "the halo of glory that now envelops
Buffalo Bill." The same journalist pointed out
that an American who got into trouble in France
must seek help from the American minister, as
the ambassador was called at that time. "[B]ut for
real distinction," he added, "you must proclaim
yourself a countryman of Buffalo Bill."

Yet James Gordon Bennett Jr., the American
publisher of the Paris *Herald*, found to his
dismay that the French still needed some
educating about America. Not long after the

Wild West show opened, eight outraged Paris councilmen said that it should be shut down because the black and Indian members of the company were slaves. Not one member of the council seemed to know that there had been no slaves in America since the Civil War (1861–65). But another French politician explained that there was no need to take away Parisians' favorite entertainment, because the poor Wild West slaves became free once they landed on French soil.

"This is simply excruciating," Bennett sputtered. "It quite paralyzes us, and renders comment impossible." Ignorance about America irritated Bennett. He was an ardent patriot. As he explained to a Paris editor, "I love America, but I hate most Americans."

The phenomenal success of Buffalo Bill's Wild West in Paris should not have been a complete surprise. The show had conquered London just two summers earlier. Many Americans knew that the Prince of Wales, heir to the throne, had persuaded Queen Victoria that she had to see the Wild West and its amazing exhibitions.

The queen was head of the vast British Empire at the height of its power. Still, as the prince expected, she had been as delighted and fascinated by the whoop-it-up performance as any child. Afterward, she had stunned everyone by insisting on personally greeting Buffalo Bill, the Sioux chief Red Shirt, and Annie Oakley. "You are a very, very clever girl," the queen told Oakley.

England had been electrified to learn that a second royal performance was ordered. This time, Buffalo Bill drove the stagecoach and assigned the Prince of Wales to ride with him. Royals from Denmark, Greece, Belgium, and Saxony (now part of Germany) held on for dear life inside the coach as it careened about, "escaping" the marauding Indians. And now, two years after conquering London, the Wild West was making another conquest, in Paris.

The Real U.S. Ambassador

The real American ambassador in France was Whitelaw Reid, the publisher of the *New-York Tribune*. Reid was new to the post—he had arrived in Paris the day after Buffalo Bill.

Reid had made a name for himself as a journalist covering the American Civil War. He had bought the *Tribune* in 1872. Its circulation

BLACK ELK'S RETURN

A SURPRISE OCCURRED DURING THE EARLY WEEKS at the Wild West camp. Black Elk suddenly arrived.

Black Elk was a Sioux holy man who had been with the show when it toured England two years earlier. When the time had come for the company to board the steamship for the journey back to America, Black Elk had failed to appear at the dock.

It turned out that he and several other Indians stranded in England had spent the time since then touring around Europe with an outfit called Mexican Joe's, a third-rate version of Cody's Wild West show. By the time Mexican Joe's played in Paris earlier that year, Black Elk was too ill to perform. A French family took him in and nursed him as best they could.

Black Elk was in a coma for three days. When
he woke, the family told him that Buffalo Bill was
in town. "So they took me to where he had his
show, and he was glad to see me," Black Elk said.
"He had all his people give me three cheers. Then
he asked me if I wanted to be in the show or if I
wanted to go home. I told him I was sick to go
home. So he said he would fix that."

Cody, said the Indian, had "a big heart." He
gave Black Elk a steamship ticket and some
money, and then hosted a big farewell dinner for
him. Soon Black Elk was crossing the Atlantic, on
his way home.

was smaller than those of some other well-known American newspapers of the day, but it appealed to literary people and to influential Republican readers.

Ten years after buying the paper, Reid had married the daughter of a gold rush millionaire. This raised him into the ranks of the very rich. In the previous presidential election, Reid had successfully persuaded Republicans to drive Democrat Grover Cleveland out of the White House by electing Republican Benjamin Harrison. Reid had hoped that his help would lead Harrison to make him the new U.S. ambassador to England. Reluctantly, he had had to settle for France.

After meeting with Sadi Carnot, the president of France, Reid wrote to President Harrison that Carnot had "a kindly feeling [toward America] because of our attitude towards their exposition while Europe was boycotting it."

At that meeting, Reid had said to Carnot, "We do not forget that you helped in the success of our Revolution." True, the French monarchy had once lent money to save the American republic being born out of revolutionary British colonies. But France had done so to help break up the

British Empire, its "hated and powerful rival," as Alexander Hamilton, one of America's Founding Fathers, had put it.

Over time, the myth had taken hold that the eighteenth-century French monarchy had helped the American revolutionaries out of love for the idea of liberty. It was now up to the United States to support the new French Republic that had replaced that monarchy—and Americans could strengthen the fragile republic by spending a lot of American dollars.

Reid reported that there was no sign of the Paris fair being a failure. "Americans have been swarming here as if Paris were another Oklahoma," he wrote, referring to the land rush that same year that drew thousands of settlers into the Territory of Oklahoma. New American arrivals in Paris hurried to the office of the *Herald* to sign a list of visitors. They greeted one another with cries of "Why, when did you come?"

Although he had come to Paris only out of duty to the Republican Party, Minister Reid found the French friendly. Still, he quickly learned that an American ambassador ranked low in the pecking order of international diplomats. When he went to call on a French

minister about some young American women
who had gotten in trouble over an unpaid bill,
Reid had to wait while ambassadors from Russia,
Germany, Turkey, Austria, and Italy (who had
arrived after him) were seen first.

Overall, Reid found the colony of Americans
in Paris in a fine mood. Everyone was puffed up
with pride, feeling patriotic over the triumphs of
Buffalo Bill and the Edison Company, and looking
forward to a summer of pleasure at the fair.

Whitelaw Reid,
c. 1880.

CHAPTER EIGHT

ART WARS

Competition as well as fellowship was in the air at the 1889 Universal Exposition. The realm of art was no exception. In the field of the arts, there was competition between nations, rivalry between artists, and conflict between buyers and sellers.

Apart from the Eiffel Tower, no subject stirred up as much ill will and trouble between France and the United States as fine art. And it all boiled to the surface when buyers from the two nations fought over a treasured French painting.

The Precious Prize

It was Monday, July 1. Everyone who was anyone in Paris was not at the fair or on the Eiffel

Exhibition of art at the
Paris Expoisition, 1889.

Tower. Instead, people crowded anxiously into an art gallery in the rustic part of Paris known as Montmartre. Carriages lined the curbs for blocks around. Even the most elegant ladies and gentlemen had trouble pushing through to their reserved seats.

The gallery was soon to be the scene of an eagerly awaited art sale. A man named Hyacinth Secrétan had made a fortune buying and selling copper. He had bought hundreds of works of art, including some very famous paintings. And then the price of copper collapsed, and Secrétan's fortune collapsed with it. He had vanished, leaving only his spectacular art collection to be sold to pay his debts.

Everyone at the gallery knew that the auction's biggest prize was *The Angelus*, a painting by a Frenchman named Jean-François Millet. And everyone also knew that either a French or an American buyer would depart with that prize. The air was electric with the energy of cultural combat. The auction was about to show the world just how angry France's cultural leaders had become about Americans making off with French treasures.

French Against Americans

When it came to Americans and art, the French had mixed feelings.

French artists were delighted to sell their works to rich Americans, and jacked up their prices when doing so. French painters were happy to have American students pay to study in their studios. However, as their number grew, American artists living in Paris wanted to show their work at the yearly Salon, the top art show in the country. This, to the French, was a different matter. They began to resent foreigners taking up valuable exhibition space.

One person who had come to the crowded gallery for the auction in Montmartre was the French minister of fine arts, Antonin Proust. He had played a big part in the organization of the Paris fair. Proust had suffered no end of complaining from French artists over who had been chosen for the official national exhibit, how many paintings each could hang, and why this painting or that did not have a better spot. No truer words had been spoken than Proust's comment: "The secret of satisfying everybody has not yet been discovered."

THE STORY OF *THE ANGELUS*

IN THE CATHOLIC CHURCH, THE ANGELUS IS A devotion, or prayer, that the faithful perform at certain hours. The ringing of a church bell is the signal for the prayer. *The Angelus*, the painting that caused so much strong feeling at the 1889 auction, had been completed by Jean-François Millet between 1857 and 1859. There was a wonderful story behind it.

According to an article that appeared in the *Washington Post* a few days after the auction, Millet was walking home one day when he heard a church bell. Just then he saw, "across the wide stretch of autumn fields, against the crimson sky of sunset, two peasants, a man and a woman, stop instantly from their potato digging at the sound of the Angelus and devoutly fall to prayer." Millet rushed to his studio to paint the scene.

Paris, 1909.

That is not, however, the only story about the painting. According to a French museum, Millet said, "The idea for *The Angelus* came to me because I remembered that my grandmother, hearing the church bell ringing while we were working in the fields, always made us stop work to say the Angelus prayer for the poor departed."

In the twentieth century, painter Salvador Dalí suggested that the painting showed a funeral scene: a young couple praying over their dead baby. This idea was unpopular, but eventually the Louvre, France's great art museum, had the painting X-rayed. The scan revealed a small shape like a coffin next to the basket of potatoes. The image had been painted over.

Perhaps the true story of *The Angelus* is not yet known.

On this day, Proust was determined to outbid the Americans for *The Angelus* and keep Millet's masterpiece in France. He had single-handedly raised 400,000 francs to buy the painting. He expected that if he had to bid more, France's government would make up the difference so that the painting could hang in the Louvre.

To the distress of the French, half the people who had come for the sale were Americans. Many of them were absurdly wealthy. In recent years, the French government had become concerned about the flow of art across the Atlantic Ocean. An investigator had been sent to the United States and had reported, "I would never have believed, had I not confirmed it myself, that the United States, so young a country, could be so rich in works of painting, especially works of the French school. It is not by the hundreds but by the thousands that one must count them."

Onlookers that day recognized several American millionaires or the representatives who would bid on their behalf. The French stared with open loathing at the Americans who dared to carry off the art gems of France.

American Art Association (AAA) founder James Sutton attended the auction. Word had spread of the "thrilling story" of Sutton's arrival—how his ship had landed late, how he had hired a special train, and how he had raced to Paris to be on time for this very sale. Now he was rumored to have a special train waiting to carry him to a steamship the instant he had bagged *The Angelus*. Next to him sat a French agent named Montagnac, who had been hired to make the AAA's bids.

The Auction

At about one o'clock, the auction began. The gallery's managers worked steadily through the lesser items from the collection of the vanished Secrétan. Next, they brought out major paintings by the French artists Eugène Delacroix and Ernest Meissonier. Fabulous prices were paid for these.

At last, after a brief pause, a gallery man carried out *The Angelus* and reverently placed it on an easel. Proust, the French fine arts minister, stood up and walked forward to bid personally against the AAA's Montagnac.

The French seemed to be in agony as the

bids soared higher and higher. At one point, Montagnac faltered. An American in the crowd stood up and said, "If you haven't money enough, I'll stand by you." The French made the same offer to Proust, who by now was white-faced and trembling with emotion. Then Montagnac bid again, and the auctioneer's hammer crashed down—the Americans had won.

There was an uproar as the French leaped furiously to their feet. Women broke their fans in anger. The bidding was reopened. This time Proust was the winner. When the hammer came down, he had just paid the highest price on record at that time for a modern painting: 550,000 francs, or $110,000. The French rushed forward and surrounded him as if he were a conquering hero.

As calm returned, the auction resumed. It would continue into the next day. Many French people who were in the audience noted unhappily how often the American millionaires won the bidding. The Americans may have missed out on *The Angelus*, but they would carry other prized paintings back across the Atlantic.

The Millet Controversy

Everyone in the art world knew that the issue of money to pay Proust's bid on the Millet painting was politically controversial. Conservatives in France and in its government were working to end the republic and bring back the monarchy. This right-wing faction was hostile to Millet, whom they considered a left-wing communist. They disliked his painting because it was an image of poor peasants—common people rather than aristocrats, war heroes, or historical figures. But the proud Proust assumed that his fellow Frenchmen, whatever their politics, would not tolerate Americans making off with such a famous painting.

As soon as the auction ended, Proust gave his request for the money to the Chamber of Deputies, which had to release the funds. For two weeks, the deputies debated the matter. The days passed, and still the conservative deputies blocked the credit that Proust needed to complete the purchase of *The Angelus*. He agonized once again over the prospect of losing the painting to the Americans.

General Rush Hawkins, the commissioner of the American art exhibition, watched this *Angelus* affair with displeasure. He did not think much of the painting. To Hawkins (and many others), Millet's work may have been realistic, but it was crude and uninteresting. "[Millet's] subjects, as a rule, were unworthy of a great master," Hawkins wrote, adding that "his human types nearly express idiots or monsters."

Not everyone agreed with this harsh verdict on Millet and his work. Painter Vincent van Gogh had followed the news of the auction and wrote to his brother Theo, "I am always pleased that the Millets hold their own. But I should very much like to see more good reproductions of Millet, so as to reach the people. His work is sublime."

By the middle of July, the sunny summer days had been blown away by heavy winds, followed by days of cold, rainy weather. This suited the mood of Proust, the minister of fine arts. He had won the bidding war, but by now he knew that there was no hope he would be able to buy *The Angelus* for France.

Conservatives in the Chamber of Deputies had permanently set aside a bill to finance the purchase of the painting. Millet and his subjects were too close to republican hearts. After his frenzied moment of triumph at the auction, Proust had to officially give up his prize and watch James Sutton of the American Art Association sail off with it.

The Americans had won *The Angelus*. Frustrating as this must have been to Proust and others who had hoped to keep the painting in France, the United States had it for only a short time. The very next year, the American Art Association sold the painting to a French collector, who later gave it to the French state. It hung in the Louvre from 1909 until 1986, when it was moved to another Paris museum.

American Gold

On July 16, in spite of a steady drizzle outside, joy reigned at the headquarters of the American art exhibition. General Rush Hawkins had received good news. He immediately shared it with James Gordon Bennett Jr.'s Paris *Herald*. The 255 American artists who had shown work at the fair had won a total of 108 medals.

This was a huge relief, after rumors that the juries had seen little to impress them on the crowded walls of the American galleries.

"Our countrymen will doubtless be surprised," Hawkins said. He felt Americans had reason to be proud. It was the first time American artists had competed directly with "the artists of the world."

Three Americans had won the highest award, the Medal of Honor. Two were painters (John Singer Sargent and J. Gari Melchers). The third was sculptor Paul Wayland Bartlett. Another seven artists had won gold medals. Americans would have taken home eight gold medals if James McNeill Whistler had not chosen to exhibit his work with the British. He had received a gold medal for his portrait of Lady Archibald Campbell, an old friend.

Whistler, in London, was pleased about his gold medal. He graciously accepted congratulations from his French friends, even though he viewed the honor as inevitable. The many enemies Whistler had made over the years thought it was "a horror" that he had won over more deserving English artists. Some American art critics, though, swooned with admiration. They declared Whistler a brilliant and original painter.

At the time, Whistler was embroiled in a legal fight. A London brewer had hired him to paint a portrait of his wife, but Whistler had destroyed it after the wife complained that it was taking too long. Whistler was an expert at using scandal to keep people talking about him. The legal fight together with the gold medal in Paris were very useful in drawing crowds to see his work—and in selling it.

The Artists and the Fair

General Rush Hawkins had survived many rounds of combat in the American Civil War. He felt pleased and grateful to come out of the Paris art wars bruised but victorious.

He had put up with a lot of complaining from his own artists, followed by more grumbling from American art critics. One complaint was that the U.S. painters had failed to get across "a national story, a national landscape and a moral elevation." In other words, the American paintings were not American enough or refined enough. While the Americans had held their own at the fair, the fact was that the French juries had simply rewarded them for studying and painting in Paris.

The cranky Hawkins had to write an official report of the American art show at the fair. He took advantage of the opportunity to criticize troublesome individuals, including Whistler. He called Whistler's prizewinning portrait of Lady Campbell "in no respect satisfactory."

The American artists of Paris, in turn, had plenty to say about Hawkins. By late summer they were still venting their anger at him in the pages of the Paris *Herald*. They complained about the makeup of the art juries, the placement of the artists' works, and more.

When the artists of all nationalities were not squabbling about whose work deserved to be displayed or to win medals, many of them were actually painting and sketching the astonishing sights of the fair. Paul Signac, a French architecture student, was the first. He painted the Eiffel Tower when it was half-finished. A young artist named Henri Rivière spent hours sketching the tower and its surroundings. He showed workers laboring in all seasons to build the tower, as well as the finished tower from many viewpoints.

Henri Rousseau, a self-taught artist who worked in the Paris Customs Office, painted a charming portrait of himself with the Eiffel Tower in the background, the French flag at its pinnacle. Rousseau was so taken with the tower that he wrote a three-act vaudeville show called *Une visite à l'Exposition 1889* ("A Visit to the 1889 Fair"). It told of a family of French country bumpkins on a trip to see the Eiffel Tower and the other marvels of the fair.

After the Eiffel Tower, the fair subject that most attracted French artists was the dancing girls from Java, in what is now Indonesia. Major artists such as Paul Gauguin, Camille Pissarro, Auguste Rodin, and Henri de Toulouse-Lautrec all sketched or painted them. So did American Medal of Honor winner John Singer Sargent. The Paris fair was a rich source of inspiration, not just irritation, for its artists.

CHAPTER NINE

THE FOURTH
OF JULY

BY THE MIDDLE OF SUMMER, MOST OF THE
writers and artists who had once criticized
the tower had admitted that they were wrong.
One exception was the French author Guy de
Maupassant, who wrote, "I left Paris and even
France, because the Eiffel Tower just annoyed
me too much. Not only did you see it from
everywhere; you found it everywhere made out
of every known material, displayed in all the
shop windows, an unavoidable and horrible
nightmare."

But Maupassant and his opinion were now
very much in the minority. Most days, even
during bad weather, thousands of people
swarmed around the tower. It was proving

Entrance to one of the
Otis Elevators.

to be more than a technological milestone. It was a powerful political symbol of the French Republic, a success with the country's people, and a financial triumph.

A number of celebrities were smitten with the tower. Sarah Bernhardt, the most famous woman in Paris and the greatest actress of her time, was a visitor. Auguste Bartholdi, the sculptor of the Statue of Liberty, also paid a call. The city's most stylish people and its intellectuals flocked to the restaurants in the tower. Before he fled Paris, even Guy de Maupassant found he had no choice—he had to visit the tower if he wanted to socialize with his friends, who were holding dinner parties there instead of in their homes.

On July 2, a leading French intellectual, publisher Edmond de Goncourt, dined with other writers on the Eiffel Tower. He later described going up in the elevator as "the sensation of a vessel putting out to sea." Being on a platform, he said, gave "a perception, far beyond one's thinking at ground level, of the grandeur, the size, the Babylonian immensity of Paris."

An American Holiday

Buffalo Bill Cody's Wild West was a little piece of America in the heart of France. It was only right, then, that the Fourth of July, the anniversary of America's independence, would be a day of special celebrations there.

The morning dawned blue and warm. Everyone at the show was up early to hang French and American flags. The company assembled while the Cowboy Band played lively versions of the patriotic songs "Yankee Doodle" and "Hail, Columbia." Then Nate Salsbury stepped forward to read aloud the Declaration of Independence, as he did every year. As he finished, the Americans began to holler and applaud. Buffalo Bill then offered a few patriotic remarks.

Cody, Salsbury, and a few others then hurried into a horse-drawn carriage to go to the next event of the day. After an hour's ride, they reached a high-walled cemetery off a small street in southeast Paris. There they joined several hundred Americans (including thirty U.S. Marines) who had come to pay tribute to a French military hero, General Lafayette. During the American Revolution, Lafayette had fought

THE PANAMA CRASH

IN THE MIDDLE OF THE PLEASURES AND excitements of the Universal Exposition, one great disappointment disturbed Gustave Eiffel. While the fair was showing the world the power of France's industrial spirit, the Panama Canal, France's ambitious plan to remake the map of the world, was in its death throes.

The Panama Canal Company had collapsed fully into bankruptcy. Eiffel reluctantly told his laborers in Panama to stop work on the locks he had designed. In July his contract ended. Throughout France, families were devastated by the loss of money they had invested in the canal. The undertaking had been a financial disaster.

Panama, 1911.

Eiffel had thought that the Panama Canal would be his last great work. He expected it to be another colossal engineering project for the glory of France, one that would outshine the Eiffel Tower. Alas, that was not to be. But Eiffel could not have imagined how much misery the canal project's failure would cause him just a few years in the future.

on the side of the revolutionaries, which made him a hero to the United States as well.

To reach Lafayette's simple grave, the Americans threaded past the tombs of many French aristocrats who had been beheaded on the guillotine during the French Revolution a century earlier. Soon Lafayette's tomb had disappeared beneath the bouquets and wreaths the Americans had brought.

Minister Reid, the American ambassador to France, said a few words. Senator Edmond de Lafayette, the general's grandson, thanked the Americans for honoring his ancestor. The ceremony ended with volleys of shots from the marines and the mournful sound of their bugle.

"Exceedingly Good Terms"

The Fourth of July celebration in Paris continued on the bank of the Seine. As the river shimmered in the summer sunlight and the barges passed, Minister Reid and several thousand Americans were joined by President Carnot of France and hundreds of uniformed French officials. Buffalo Bill and Chief Rocky Bear squeezed in to watch.

The Americans who lived in Paris were presenting a gift to the Republic of France. It was a copy of the Statue of Liberty that France had given to the United States. This bronze gift was one-fifth the size of the original, which stands in New York Harbor.

From the start, the 1889 Universal Exposition had held a strong element of competition between France and the United States. But for this day, rivalry had given way to friendship between the nations. As an American reporter wrote, "Altogether, Paris and America are on exceedingly good terms with one another."

Minister Reid was delighted to see that the fair was a roaring success. He felt that the exhibits and all the socializing they brought about helped build stronger ties between France and the United States. As Buffalo Bill and the others from the Wild West show rode their carriage back to their camp for their afternoon performance, they saw a rare sight. The French flag normally flew from the top of the Eiffel Tower. On this day, though, the tower flew the American Stars and Stripes for three hours, in honor of the United States' Independence Day.

All Are Welcome

That evening, a crush of Americans jammed a fashionable Paris street. They were there for Minister Reid's Fourth of July open house and celebration. The Reids had just moved into one of the city's legendary private mansions, and Americans who lived in Paris were dying for a look inside.

Mrs. Reid greeted the throng wearing a large diamond necklace and a black-and-white-striped silk gown. The curiosity seekers were not disappointed. The rented mansion had four formal, mirrored drawing rooms and a dining room that could seat twenty-four people, decorated in crimson fabric.

The Reids' party turned tradition on its head. For years, Americans in Paris—that is, the select few who were invited—had celebrated the Fourth of July at the magnificent home of Dr. Thomas Evans, a Philadelphia dentist who had moved to Paris in 1847, at the age of twenty-four. His ability to ease pain had earned him the business and gratitude of royalty across Europe. He became extremely wealthy and built a palatial marble mansion furnished with luxurious gifts from his royal patients. It was set in a park with fountains, rose gardens, American trees, and aviaries full of rare and colorful birds.

Evans was a royalist—he favored monarchies and hoped that France's new republican government would not last. American diplomats working in Paris resented him for two reasons. First, he had more contact with the nobility of Europe than they had. Second, no U.S. minister had ever been able to afford to live or entertain as splendidly as Evans did. In the American community in Paris, invitations to Evans's Fourth of July celebration were prized as a sign of one's high status.

But Minister Reid had done something unheard of. He had issued an open invitation to all Americans to come to his celebration. Many of the Americans who lived in Paris, and all the diplomats, were delighted.

Reid's democratic invitation also pleased newspaperman James Gordon Bennett, who wrote in his Paris *Herald,* "We offer our hearty congratulations to the United States Minister for the wise step taken in the way of invitations. Instead of making a great stir and commotion by drawing up 'visiting lists' . . . and causing heart-burnings and tempests in teapots, Mr.

Whitelaw Reid simply reverted to the old ways of Washington and Jefferson and Adams. All Americans were informed they were welcome to the Minister's home. And they went there, and they enjoyed themselves."

The Reids' party was a great success. A thousand Americans of every class and position in life happily inspected the mansion and one another. One of the guests, Buffalo Bill Cody, wrote to his favorite sister, Julia, that he had had a busy day on the Fourth and had finally gone to bed at daylight.

A Challenge from the French

Right after the Fourth of July, Buffalo Bill received a challenge. The Wild West show featured an act in which a cowboy rode and tamed a wild bronco. The French equestrian set—people involved in breeding, riding, and racing horses—questioned whether the performers could really do such a thing. They decided to put it to the test.

A member of the elite Jockey Club owned what Cody called a "fiery untamed steed." He proposed that during a regular Wild West performance, this "wild colt shall be lassoed, saddled and ridden within the time usually given to the bucking show of the set." Colonel Cody agreed.

On July 8, the fine-looking black stallion was delivered to the corral next to the Wild West arena. Word of the challenge had gotten out. A huge crowd jammed the stands. Much of the Jockey Club was present, in ringside boxes. There was heavy betting.

Buffalo Bill told his cowboys that the horse was to be captured, ridden, and quieted—but gently, and without any cruelty or injury to the horse. Jim Kidd won the honor of riding the stallion. First, though, Buffalo Bill would lasso and saddle the horse.

When the time came, Cody lassoed the horse on the first try. Saddling it gave him great trouble, but he did it. Jim Kidd sprang into the saddle. Off charged the stallion, bucking furiously. The *Chicago Tribune* described what happened next:

> *No other horse has ever pawed so much air under a cowboy. Once he tried to jump over the stand. But Kidd kept his seat and presently had the horse under so much control that he*

A TAX WAR OVER PORK AND ART

AFTER THE FOURTH OF JULY, U.S. MINISTER Whitelaw Reid took the warm ceremonies shared by French and Americans as a good sign for his overall mission. His main challenge was to persuade France to remove its tariff on American pork. (A tariff is a special tax on goods that are imported into or exported from a country.) France had placed a tariff on pork coming into the country from the United States, but the reason may have had to do with wine.

France had long been famous for its wines, and for the vineyards of grapes from which the wines were made. In the second half of the nineteenth century, those vineyards had been attacked by a

Paris Exposition, 1889.

destructive pest, a type of plant-eating aphid. The French had discovered that the pest had almost certainly come from the United States.

After that, France placed a high tariff on American pork, which made the pork so expensive in France that no one imported it. This amounted to a ban on pork from the United States. French authorities claimed that the tariff was meant to protect the French people from trichinosis, a disease that can be carried in pork, but many Americans believed it was just revenge for the wine-destroying pest. U.S. farmers' earnings from pork exports to France dropped from $4 million in 1881 to just $5,000 in 1888

because of the tariff.

The United States had not taken France's pork tariff lying down. In 1883, it placed a tariff on art from France that was imported into the United States. One French artist complained that it was strange for a government to tax "products of the mind." He added that works of art were free of special taxes all over the world—except in the United States.

It was Minister Reid's task to untangle this mess. He found, though, that France's politicians were too busy with the world's fair and with their own political problems to take up the issue. All he could do was suggest to the U.S. government that lowering the U.S. tariff on French art might make France more willing to do the same for American pork.

*actually took "Mother" Whittaker [the beloved
wardrobe mistress of the show] up behind, and
the two rode around the ring as the cowboy
band played "See the Conquering Hero
Comes." It was the finest specimen of riding
ever seen in Paris and the immense audience
showed its appreciation of the young man's
skill by round after round of applause.*

The Wild West show had proven itself
handsomely. The French loss was not just a
matter of pride. One member of the Jockey Club
was said to have lost a small fortune betting
against the Americans.

An Offer for Annie Oakley

Annie Oakley was having a wondrous Paris
summer. Her shooting skills were widely
admired. President Sadi Carnot had told her,
"When you feel like changing your nationality
and profession there is a commission waiting for
you in the French Army."

On July 12, Oakley received a different kind
of offer. The king of the Nalu people of the West
African nation of Guinea, Dinah Salifou, had
come to the Wild West show from his home in

Annie Oakley with
some of the medals
she won in sharp-
shooting contests.

exile in Senegal with his veiled wives and his twelve-year-old princely son. King Salifou was greatly impressed by Annie Oakley's blasting of glass balls and other flying objects.

After the show, King Salifou sought out Buffalo Bill in the campground. He said how much he admired the sharpshooter and then asked Cody, "How much do you want for her?"

"Want for her?" Cody said. "What do you mean?"

"To sell her," the king replied. "I wish to take her back with me." He explained that he would like Oakley to be his "chief huntress" and kill the man-eating animals that menaced people in some of the villages in his country.

When the situation was explained to her, Oakley said to Cody, "But am I for sale, Colonel?"

"Come to think of it, I guess you ain't," he answered.

The king raised his price, but Cody put an end to the joke. He told the king that Oakley was no slave but her own person, a modern woman, and a citizen of the United States. The king knelt, kissed her hand, and departed "with the air of a soldier," as Oakley later said.

King Salifou's presence at the fair was a piece of French politicking. Traders and others from France had been present in Senegal for a long time, and now the republic wanted Senegal, where the king lived, as a colony. The French government had invited the African king to its fair to advance France's empire-building plans. All kinds of national ambitions lurked beneath the pleasures and accomplishments of the fair.

Annie Oakley.

CHAPTER TEN

MONARCHS OF
THE WORLD

A DEEP TENSION RAN THROUGH THE 1889
Universal Exposition, showing itself in many
ways. It was the tension of an old, traditional
form of society and government giving way to a
new one.

For most of its history, France had been a
monarchy, governed by a king, like most other
European nations and many countries in other
parts of the world. The French Revolution of
1789 had toppled the monarchy to establish a
republican state, one governed by representatives
of the citizens, with laws spelled out in a
constitution. Twice since that time, monarchy
had been briefly restored in France. Now the
country was in its Third Republic, but that

Fairgoers near the
fountain on the
Champ de Mars, with
the Central Dome in
the background.

republic was very new. It had been born less than twenty years before the fair.

The fair was meant to show that France was a strong industrial nation. The Eiffel Tower and other feats of construction proved that point. It was also meant to show that France was becoming modern and successful under a republican government, and to advance the new republic on the world stage.

Paris was noticeably more prosperous and more democratic than it had been a generation earlier. The self-made man had become an important figure. New industrial fortunes such as Eiffel's were overturning the old social order that was based on class standing and titles.

France and the United States had much in common, even though they were rivals at the fair. (Perhaps that is why they were rivals.) Both were republics. Both had democratic ideals, seeing dignity in common people and allowing all to participate in government.

When conservative politicians refused to pay for Millet's *Angelus*, a portrait of peasant life, they rejected something that conflicted with their monarchic values. But even many passionate believers in the new republican order remained fascinated by wealth, privilege, and nobility.

Most European monarchs and royals snubbed the fair and stayed away. A few showed up, as did royalty from other continents. The 1889 Universal Exposition was the most democratic and republican fair ever, yet the French government delighted in the visit of every single royal. As did Gustave Eiffel.

Royal Roll Call

High above Paris on his tower, Eiffel found foreign nobility and royalty to be the most pleasing of visitors.

First had come the Prince of Wales, heir to the throne of Great Britain, with his family. His visit had been unofficial because his mother, Queen Victoria, had made it clear that she wanted her government to stay away from the fair.

After the British royals' visit, Eiffel had welcomed to his republican tower the former queen Isabella II of Spain. She had been forced to step down from the throne and had been exiled from Spain in 1868 because of her misrule of the country. For some time, she had been living in

Paris, but she was still a kind of royalty.

Other royals went up the Eiffel Tower that summer. They included the Duke of Edinburgh, who was also an admiral in the British navy, and Nicholas II of Russia, who would soon become czar, or supreme ruler, of that country. The khedive of Egypt, who governed that country on behalf of the Turkish Ottoman Empire, was also a visitor.

July 22 had brought to the tower the heir to the throne of Siam, today known as Thailand, along with two younger Siamese princes. The very next day, King George of Greece had visited. He ignored the heavy rain that hid the view and chose to dine in the tower's Russian restaurant because his queen had been a princess of Russia.

Later, the ambassador from Germany came to the tower. The new French Republic had come into being during a disastrous war with Germany, the Franco-Prussian War of 1870–71. The relationship between the two countries was strained, and the German government, as well as most German private businesses, had been boycotting the fair. This made the ambassador's visit a patriotic victory for France.

Eiffel's most colorful foreign visitor was

Dinah Salifou, the same king of the Nalu of Guinea who had tried to buy Annie Oakley from Buffalo Bill. He showed up with a large group of attendants and followers, including a four-man orchestra that followed him around playing background music. King Salifou and his queen later came to the tower for a second visit, this time bringing eight young princes, all of whom spoke good French. Once again, the king's musicians played at the tower's summit.

The Shah of Persia

Of all the royals who came to the fair, the most eagerly awaited visitor to the Eiffel Tower was Nasir al-Din, the Shah of Persia (what is now known as Iran). The fifty-eight-year-old shah (or king) was the descendant of an ancient emperor. He was a man of incredible wealth as well as extraordinary power in his own country. Although he was short, he made a striking impression in his colorful uniform decorated with very large precious stones. Gustave Eiffel was eager to welcome him to the tower.

On the last day of July, the shah made his first, informal visit to the fair. According to the Paris *Herald*, he went straight to the Eiffel Tower, but after climbing a few of the steps that led to the elevators, he abandoned any idea of going up. He turned around and went on to see the rest of the fair.

The shah had visited Paris twice before. His wealth, and his willingness to spend it, had made him a legend. Now, as he strolled across the fairgrounds, he made numerous purchases. One of them was a large black diamond that he bought to add to his collection of royal jewels.

After visiting the fair, the shah and his attendants traveled in a string of carriages to a palatial mansion in a large, walled park. The mansion was owned by the French Republic and had been lavishly furnished. The shah occupied the entire second floor. From the balcony off his bedroom he could see the Eiffel Tower he had refused to ascend.

Two days later, August 2, was a clear and sunny day after two weeks of rain. Everyone who worked at the tower was in a state of high excitement. An official notice had been sent that His Majesty the Shah would visit the tower that day. Reporters for *Le Figaro*, girls who sold trinkets and cigars, waiters, elevator operators— all wore their best clothes. They crowded the platform railings, waiting for the first glimpse of the royal procession. Down below, they saw only the usual crowds, dotted with the bobbing parasols that women had put up to protect their skin from the sun.

By noon, a cloud of disappointment had settled over the tower. His Majesty the Shah was not coming.

Up at Last

Royal visits to the Eiffel Tower got lots of publicity. So did the fact that the Shah of Persia had first turned back on going up the tower and then failed to show up at all. The shah was the target of some mockery.

On August 3, a *New York Times* reporter was strolling on the first platform of the tower. He stopped suddenly, unable to believe his eyes. Was this the Persian king, dressed in blue, coming up the staircase? The reporter wrote:

> To my astonishment, and the utter
> stupefaction of the bewildered authorities,
> up climbed the Shah. He had been trying to
> screw up his courage ever since his arrival,
> but had never gotten above the third step,
> and there he was, all by himself, far in

*advance of his frightened [attendants] and
looking like a very brilliant, anxious fish,
suddenly landed from deep water on high
ground. Such a funny scene of confusion I
never saw.*

Another reporter, this one from *Le Figaro*,
was right behind the shah on the stairs. He
reported that the king walked up slowly and
admired the view. He spent a long time leaning
on the balcony of the first platform, gazing at the
outspread city.

The shah, it turned out, was supposed to be
at an event in another part of Paris. All kinds
of government officials were waiting there
for him. The French republican government
was determined to show that it was as good as
royalists at holding proper ceremonies. It had
planned every possible formal occasion for the
shah, who was the first official royal state visitor
to the fair. But now here he was, wandering
around the Eiffel Tower like any tourist. "He
looked exactly like a schoolboy caught in
mischief," the *Times* reporter wrote.

A royal luncheon was quickly organized in
one of the tower cafés. Afterward, the shah

walked to the elevator to the second floor. He got into it—and then reconsidered and got out again. He headed straight for the stairs and disappeared downward. Many salespeople were disappointed. The shah had bought only two dozen tiny souvenir towers and a walking stick with a tower handle.

The King and the Cowboy

By now it had become a must for every celebrity and royal who came to the fair to attend Buffalo Bill's Wild West show. The Shah of Persia was no exception.

The Wild West camp was in a great lather preparing for the visit of this exotic ruler. Major Burke and Nate Salsbury made sure that special chairs had been installed, that there were many flowers, and that a refreshment table was ready with iced drinks and plates of fruit. The flags of Persia, France, and the United States were displayed. Buffalo Bill wore his finest Western costume. Ribbons, badges, and medals covered his chest.

When the shah walked into the arena, the packed audience rose and cheered. Once the crowd had settled down, the Cowboy Band

Wild West Indians—mainly Sioux—pose at the Neuilly camp.

struck up the Persian national anthem, followed by the anthems of the United States and France. The show's narrator, Richmond, appeared, and in moments, the cowboys and Indians were racing by at terrifying speeds. All eyes remained on the shah, who smiled and clapped. Like everyone else, he was astonished when Annie Oakley performed a new sharpshooting stunt: shooting a hole through the ace of spades playing card from ten yards away, and then splitting the card sideways with another shot.

After the show, the shah visited the campground. Buffalo Bill showed him through the teepees and tents. Before the shah left, he lived up to his reputation for generosity by giving a large sum to the entire company. He was also rumored to have given Buffalo Bill a diamond star pin. That day, a baby buffalo had been born at the camp. It was the first buffalo ever born in Europe. It was named Shah in honor of the Persian king.

Different Kinds of Royalty

Not long after the Shah of Persia's visit, another celebrity came to the Wild West show. She was not royalty, but she had been connected to

ANYTHING FOR ATTENTION

BEFORE THE FAIR OF 1889, THOMAS EDISON and Buffalo Bill were already celebrities. Gustave Eiffel was less famous than the inventor or the cowboy, but he was certainly well known, at least in France. All three of them took advantage of the fair to add to their glory and reputation. They were not the only ones. Even some ordinary citizens were determined to use the fair to win fame, if only for a moment.

All kinds of gimmicks competed for attention. On a bet, two young men in matching striped shirts took turns pushing each other in a wheelbarrow from Vienna, Austria, to Paris. They covered 750 miles (1,207 kilometers) in thirty days. Even more astonishing was the Russian soldier who rode 1,600 miles (2,575 kilometers) on horseback from Saint Petersburg, Russia, to Paris. He completed this journey also in thirty days.

Paris Exposition, 1889.

A champagne maker had the world's largest wooden cask built, then hauled it to the fair in an oxcart. Big enough to hold two hundred thousand bottles of champagne, the cask quickly became one of the sights in the Palace of Food Products. A Paris jeweler drew crowds to his shop to see a three-foot-tall Eiffel Tower encrusted with diamonds that dazzled under electric spotlights. It was priced at almost half a million dollars.

Armond-Sylvain Dorgnon came from a remote region of France where all the shepherds used stilts to move quickly about while tending their far-flung flocks. He caused a sensation by stalking about the fair on his towering wooden legs. Determined to make his mark at the Eiffel Tower, in early September, Dorgnon climbed on his stilts all the way to the second floor. The paper Le Figaro reported that this feat astonished the people on the tower. They could not understand why someone already so high in the air would need stilts.

royalty. Now she was famous in her own right.

Lillie Langtry was a thirty-five-year-old actress. As a young English society beauty, she had caught the eye of the Prince of Wales and had been in a very public relationship with him for three years. After that, she survived a divorce and hard times before becoming a star of the stage.

Two years before the fair, Langtry had become an American citizen. She had come to Paris, among other reasons, to get a gown for her next play. When she attended the Wild West show, she rode in the Deadwood stagecoach that was part of the performance.

At another performance, a man named Russell Harrison rode the stage. He sat on top, waving his hat at the crowd as the stagecoach careened around the arena. This stage rider was the son of President Benjamin Harrison. Buffalo Bill treated him to a Wild West breakfast in a tent decorated with flags, flowers, and trophies from the West. A reporter described the feast:

> Such a breakfast had the gallant Colonel prepared for his visitors as they had not eaten for many a day. Baked beans, with the flavor of savory pork, corn bread, custard pie

and ice cream. Where all these wonderful
things came from was a mystery, but there
they were, and very good they were.

Harrison had spent time in the West, seeking
his fortune in mining and ranching. Those
ventures had failed, but still he enjoyed Cody's
thrilling stories of life on the plains.

Annie Oakley had her own encounters with
royalty. She and her husband had gotten into the
habit of spending their free time at the private
shooting clubs of Paris. One day, they arrived
at a club to find two strangers shooting. They
invited Oakley to join them. Only after she had
spent an hour in their company did she learn
that one of them was Grand Duke Michael
Mikhailovich of Russia.

The Life of a Rich American
The United States had no titled noblemen or
noblewomen, but it did have the extremely rich.
These wealthy few were celebrities, too. And James
Gordon Bennett Jr. was one of them. Although he
now made his home in France, Bennett continued
to live up to his image as a free-spending, wildly
unpredictable, rich American.

Bennett had insisted from the start that his Paris *Herald* was not intended to make money. Still, it flourished during the fair and turned a profit. Even more profitable was the transatlantic cable company that Bennett had founded with John Mackay, who had made an immense fortune mining silver. The cable company allowed people to send telegrams between North America and Europe. American journalists in Paris used it to send their stories to the U.S. papers. American tourists and travelers used it to keep in touch with the folks back home.

The success of the cable company came at a good time. Bennett was living a very expensive life. In addition to two luxurious Paris apartments, he owned a country estate. There he liked to entertain barons and countesses. Like many other rich Americans, Bennett found these minor members of the European nobility irresistible. The barons and countesses, for their part, were happy to dine and drink at Bennett's expense.

Bennett also had a home on the French Riviera. This sun-washed villa on the Mediterranean coast, with famous rose gardens, was his favorite. In addition, he had a castle in Scotland, but he rarely visited it. Its primary

"Meet me under the Eiffel Tower!"

purpose was to provide game birds and eggs for Bennett's table. His three homes in the United States were kept ready at all times for his possible return, although he had not lived in any of them for years. He lived in Paris because he preferred it.

The Shah Departs

On August 10, the Shah of Persia left Paris in a final blaze of ceremony. Publisher Edmond de Goncourt wrote in his diary how the shah's behavior had irritated one of Goncourt's old friends, a niece of the emperor Napoléon Bonaparte. This friend, Princess Mathilda, had called the shah "a swine" after his visit to her home.

Goncourt and some other friends had also spent time with the shah's personal doctor, who let slip the shah's low opinion of European nobility. The doctor also told bloodcurdling tales of palace life. One story concerned a court official who had abused his office. The shah ordered the man whipped in front of him. When the man screamed too loudly, the shah asked for a cord and "proceeded very calmly to have him strangled."

Whatever the shah's habits may have been, he and other royal and noble visitors to the world's fair and the Eiffel Tower had made the French Republic and Gustave Eiffel proud indeed. After the fair, Eiffel said, "We gave the monarchies the spectacle of democracy happy by virtue of its own efforts." The happy democrats, in turn, had greatly enjoyed the spectacle of royalty.

To my good friend Salter. from Thomas A Edison Sep

CHAPTER ELEVEN

EDISON'S ADVENTURE

THE DAY AFTER THE SHAH OF PERSIA LEFT
Paris, a steamship approached the port of Le
Havre. It brought to France and to the fair a new,
modern kind of royalty: the great American
inventor Thomas Edison.

At the urging of his wife, Mina, Edison had
agreed to come see the marvels of the Universal
Exposition. It would be his first visit to Paris.
The trip was a complete surprise to everyone
outside his inner circle. He had given no public
hint of his plans.

When the French learned that Edison
was about to arrive, they were thrilled. They
revered Edison and saw his visit as a wondrous
endorsement of their fair and their country.

Thomas Edison
poses with
Monsieur Salles
atop the Eiffel
Tower.

As one French paper reported, "The famous inventor Edison has come from America to study Paris and the Exposition." An American noted that the French considered Edison "the sole inventor of the telegraph, telephone, electric light, and even electricity itself, if not the solar system as well." (In fact, of those five things, Edison was responsible only for electric light.)

Alfred Tate, the secretary whom Edison had sent to London to check up on his business associate Gouraud, had made all Edison's arrangements for his Paris stay. Tate was late arriving in Le Havre from England to meet Edison's steamship. He caught up with his boss as Edison was boarding the train to Paris. A customs officer was trying to explain, in French, that Edison had to pay a duty, or tax, on the box of cigars he carried under his arm.

Tate told the customs officer that the man with the cigars was Thomas Edison. The officer looked at the inventor with awe. Tate said to Edison, "Shake hands with him and that'll pay the duty." Edison did so. The officer made a deep bow and then escorted Edison to this train car. This little incident was a sign of how worshipfully Edison would be received in Paris.

A Huge Triumph

The unexpected arrival of the world's greatest inventor was a huge triumph in a summer of triumphs for Paris and its fair. Tate had arranged for the Edisons to stay in elegant rooms in one of the city's seventeenth-century mansions. The quarters were equipped with gold-painted furniture and velvet curtains. They were full of bustle as the bellboy kept knocking to deliver more baskets of rare flowers. The square outside was constantly crowded with people hoping to catch a glimpse of the inventor.

The afternoon after his arrival, Edison and his companions made their first visit to the fair, braving huge crowds and heat. That evening, a mob of journalists showed up at the Edisons' rooms to interview the inventor. Asked about the fair, Edison said, "It is simply overwhelming, and the Eiffel Tower surpasses anything I had imagined." He had not yet gone up the tower or seen more than a bit of the fair and the city.

Edison most enjoyed talking about his ideas and inventions. "When I was on shipboard coming over I used to sit on deck by the hour and watch the waves," he said. "It made me positively savage to think of all that power going to waste. But we'll chain it up one of these days along with Niagara Falls and the winds." Edison was right, of course. Today the power of falling water, wind, and even waves is being harnessed to produce energy.

Edison had not come across the Atlantic to Paris simply to sightsee and relax. He was a tireless promoter of the wonders of modern technology, and also a master of public relations. He planned to visit the Eiffel Tower, inspect his country's exhibit at the fair, and meet leading French scientists and engineers. But always, every step of the way, he would be advancing the Edison companies.

He was a shrewd and brilliant promoter. He had brought dozens of phonographs and hundreds of wax cylinders of recordings to play on them. He planned to deposit these around town, where journalists who had come from all over the globe to cover the fair could examine them and then write about him and his products.

For the republicans of France, Edison was the ideal example of everything they held dear. He was a hardworking, self-made, modern citizen. Paris shop windows were filled with framed photographs of the inventor. Crowds surrounded him wherever he went. Both his wife and his secretary, Tate, found the tremendous hullabaloo a bit overwhelming.

Edison on the Tower

On Edison's third day in France, the weather was crisp, clear, and cool. It was perfect for the day's main event: a visit to the Eiffel Tower.

By nine in the morning, Edison and his party had gathered at the foot of the tower. Russell Harrison and two of Mina Edison's sisters had joined the group, along with several journalists and many Edison executives and their wives.

Under his arm Edison carried a phonograph as a gift for Gustave Eiffel. Unfortunately, Eiffel (who had not known that Edison was on his way) was out of town. His sister and son-in-law, Adolphe Salles, were on hand to greet the inventor in his place.

The group rode the elevators all the way to the tower's summit. As they got out of the last elevator and marveled at the panorama of Paris unfolding all around, they were startled to hear loud howls. What strange phenomenon was this high above the rooftops? American Indians!

Major Burke had taken Chief Rocky Bear and several dozen Sioux to the tower. Now they, like everyone else in Paris, were thrilled to meet the famous inventor. On their previous visit to the fair, they had listened and spoken into his miraculous talking phonograph.

After a tour of the top platform, Salles led his guests up the tiny staircase into Eiffel's private apartment. There a host of French politicians, businessmen, musicians, and editors waited eagerly to meet Edison. Lunch was served. Music was performed, with a singer, a flutist, and a violinist playing in front of Edison's phonograph. The guests were then invited to listen as many times as they liked to the recording of their performance.

The inventor was eager to see *Le Figaro*'s newsroom in the sky. The paper's editor was more than happy to help the always hands-on Edison run the printing press. The whole group signed the paper's list of visitors and then descended to the first floor for another meal at one of the cafés. Eiffel's sister gave each of the women in Edison's group a special souvenir: a medal of the tower in a little leather case.

An American Becomes an Italian Count

A few days after Edison's visit to the tower, an English journalist named Robert Sherard came to Edison's rooms by appointment to interview him. Sherard found Edison "listening to an excitable little man who was dressed in the height of fashion and who was waving a box in his hand that looked like a jewel-case." Edison was smiling sweetly in response.

The "little man" had come "on a special mission from the King of Italy." The king had been so dazzled by the gift of a phonograph that he was awarding the title of count to the American inventor. Edison, who had been partly deaf since his teens, did not at first realize what was going on. When he finally grasped the message, he gave a hearty laugh.

Later that day, Edison asked Sherard not to let the people in America know about "that tomfoolery" about becoming a count. "They would never stop laughing at me," he said. Sherard had to admit that he had already sent the news off by telegram. This drew another laugh from Edison.

After the Italian messenger's presentation, it was Sherard's turn to interview Edison. The

inventor had spent the morning touring the fair, and now he was feeling talkative. Although Edison was so absorbed with his work that he rarely came home for dinner, he had taken note of the leisurely French way of life—the long meals, the crowds strolling along the boulevards, the men and women sipping coffee or enjoying ice cream in busy cafés. When Sherard asked him what he thought of Paris, Edison did not hold back:

> *What has struck me so far chiefly is the absolute laziness of the people over here. When do these people work? What do they work at? . . . People here seem to have established an elaborate system of loafing. These engineers who come to see me, fashionably dressed, with walking sticks in their hands, when do they do their work? I can't understand it at all.*

What made it especially mystifying was that France was the world's fourth most important industrial nation, with the United States just ahead, in third place.

(previous)
Interior of the Galerie des Machines.

268

Honors for Edison

One highlight of Edison's time in Paris was
being welcomed to the seat of government
by President Sadi Carnot. The *New York Sun*
reported that "Edison has had a reception in
Paris such as no American or foreigner has ever
received."

Although Edison had not attended the 1878
Universal Exposition in Paris, his original,
primitive phonograph had been exhibited there.
Because of it, he had been made a chevalier in
the Legion of Honor. This had entitled him to
wear a red ribbon on his jacket. Now, in a formal
ceremony, Carnot raised Edison to the rank of
officer in the Legion. This meant that he, like
Eiffel, could wear a red rosette in his buttonhole.

Government officials, scientific societies,
and businesses such as the Paris Telephone
Company organized banquets to honor the
inventor. Edison was more than happy to accept
their invitations. He viewed these eight-course
meals as perfect opportunities to promote
the new Edison phonograph to audiences
of influential people. And so, each banquet
featured a demonstration of the improved,
miraculous device.

WE'LL BUILD A TALLER TOWER

MINA EDISON INVITED JOURNALIST ROBERT
Sherard, the Italian messenger, and a few others
to join the Edisons for lunch. What better spot
than a café on the Eiffel Tower? Off they went in a
horse-drawn carriage.

Sherard later wrote that his meal with Edison
on the Eiffel Tower was one of the most pleasant
he had ever shared. He sat next to Edison, and
the two had a far-ranging conversation.

Sherard asked what Edison thought of the Eiffel
Tower. One guest sniffed, "The work of a mere
bridge builder."

"No. It is a great idea," Edison said. "The
Tower is a great idea. The glory of Eiffel is in the

magnitude of the conception and the nerve in
the execution. . . . I like the French. They have
big conceptions. . . . What Englishman would
have had this idea? What Englishman could have
conceived the Statue of Liberty?"

Sherard asked, "Will you beat the tower in New
York?"

"We'll build one of 2,000 feet," Edison replied.

Minister Whitelaw Reid, who spoke decent French, attended the banquets to speak for Edison. Reid pointed out that Edison could speak for himself when he wanted, saying, "[I]ndeed, so fond is he of the sound of his own voice that he has spent months upon months devising a mechanical method of making it immortal. . . . His works speak for him." Reid took the opportunity to point out to his French hosts that America's first minister to France, Benjamin Franklin, had been another giant in the field of electrical study.

Edison was recognized and cheered everywhere he went. One night, the Edisons went to the opera. The orchestra played "The Star-Spangled Banner," and the audience, applauding and cheering, turned to look at the Edisons. Edison bowed, the audience stared at him and his companions, and only then did the opera begin.

As Edison told Robert Sherard, even he was astounded by the sheer number of people wanting a piece of his time, or money. He received hundreds of letters from people wanting loans or asking for his help with what he called "some lunatical invention of theirs."

One man who wrote several times, said Edison, had "invented an electrical toothbrush or some such nonsense."

When Edison was not attending banquets or promoting his inventions and businesses, he managed to do some sightseeing with his wife and their friends. They toured the galleries of French paintings at the fair. Later, they took in the many art treasures of the Louvre. Edison admired the French paintings he saw at the fair, calling them "grand art" because they were modern. "I think nothing of the pictures in the Louvre," he said. "I have no use for old things; they are wretched old things." For Edison, modernity was everything.

He made several art purchases at the fair. One was a painting of a young woman sitting up in bed reading the newspaper. He and Mina would display it with pride in their home. Edison was especially fond of sculpture and enjoyed walking through the sculpture galleries. He paid $1,700 for a piece called *The Genius of Electricity*. It was a two-foot-tall white marble statue of a sprite holding up a working light bulb. It would sit on the desk in his laboratory for years.

The artist who had created the painting

the Edisons bought was A. A. Anderson, an American businessman who had been living and painting in Paris for ten years. He portrayed Edison listening to his perfected phonograph. Edison confided to the painter, "Anderson, I am never so happy as when I sit down to a ten-course dinner between two Frenchmen who cannot speak a word of English."

One of the most lavish affairs held in Edison's honor was hosted by *Le Figaro*. It took place in the mansion that served as the paper's main office. The evening was ablaze with electric lights, which illuminated the colorful guests, including two famous bullfighters, a prince, and Buffalo Bill, "also glittering in his well-known costume of white and gold, topped by his ten-gallon hat."

The guests were entertained by singers, musicians, and a comedy star who pretended to be a penniless inventor. He showed an instrument that he pretended could translate French into English. It produced this sentence: "Edison is a king of the Republic of the Mind. Mankind is grateful to him." Later, of course, Edison demonstrated his phonograph and used it to entertain the crowd.

The Two Most Famous Americans in Paris
Thomas Edison had displaced Buffalo Bill as
the most talked-about American in Paris. If the
Paris fair was a showcase for the triumph of
technology, republican democracy, and a new,
modern way of life, then Edison was happy to
present himself and his products as symbols
of those virtues. Still, a visit to the Wild West
show remained a must-do for every visitor to the
world's fair, including Edison.

On the day after the lavish event at the offices
of *Le Figaro*, Edison and his companions were
treated to a late-morning Western-style "grub
steak" breakfast at Buffalo Bill's camp in Neuilly.
The eighteen-course meal was richly American.
The menu included such favorites as "Pork and
Boston baked beans," "Chicken, Maryland style,"
and "Green corn." To Edison's utter delight, it
also included something he had much missed:
two kinds of pie (apple and pumpkin).

That afternoon, as Buffalo Bill and the
painted Indians galloped out to start the show,
the crowd spied Edison. Just as at the opera, they
leaped to their feet roaring his name. At the end
of the performance they again cheered Edison,
and then hung around hoping to catch a glimpse

Buffalo Bill (fourth from left in suit, holding cane) poses with the Deadwood Stage and various Wild West performers. Major Burke is behind Cody, on the front coach step.

of him. A crowd of French admirers followed the Edison party as it toured the camp.

When they came to Annie Oakley's tent, she asked Edison if he might invent an electric gun, one that would not need gunpowder. (Perhaps she was remembering how she had had to smuggle her gunpowder into France.) He said, "I have not come to that yet, but it may come." Then he signed Oakley's autograph album.

Meeting Great Men

During his time in Paris, Edison was able to meet and spend time with people *he* admired. He made a journey to a southwest suburb of Paris to see Pierre-Jules-César Janssen, a physicist and astronomer.

Janssen was famous for documenting eclipses of the sun. In 1870 he had made a daring escape by balloon from Paris, which was surrounded by Prussian armies, so that he could cross the Mediterranean to Algeria in order to see a solar eclipse. (The weather turned out to be too cloudy to see it.)

Now Janssen ran France's National Observatory from an old palace that the government had given to him. Edison later said, "He occupied three

Wild West performers pose before the Western backdrop.

CLOWNING AROUND WITH THE INDIANS

COLONEL CODY'S WILD WEST SHOW HAD become such a beloved part of Paris that it inspired a comic spoof. The clowns at a Paris circus worked up a parody of the show called Kachalo-Ball.

The real Wild West Indians instantly gave the circus parody their stamp of approval: they came to the show in groups each night. The Indians cheered wildly as the French clowns mockingly imitated their riding, their wars, and their attacks. When the clowns took to dancing comic versions of Sioux war dances, the Native Americans in the audience laughed so hard that tears ran down their faces.

rooms, and there were 300. He had the grand dining-room for his laboratory."

Another day, Sir John Pender came to see Edison in the inventor's rooms in Paris. Edison described Pender, an inventor of telegraph equipment, as "the master of the cable system of the world at that time." Four years earlier, Pender had threatened to sue Edison over a patent. But that was in the past, and the two men went together for a walk in the fresh air. Pender laughed a great deal at Edison's American stories, and apparently wanted more of Edison's company. "For three days after," said Edison, "I could not get rid of him." Edison finally sent Pender off with a promise to visit him at his home near London before returning to the United States.

Edison most enjoyed the time he spent with Louis Pasteur, another genius with a practical side. Edison had invented revolutionary technologies and new businesses. Pasteur was a brilliant chemist who had come up with the revolutionary theory that diseases were caused by germs. He had used this discovery to invent pasteurization (making food immensely safer), to save the French silkworm industry, and to develop vaccines for several diseases.

Just three years before the fair, Pasteur had caused a sensation when he saved the lives of several people who had been bitten by rabid dogs. He had developed the first treatment for the condition. More recently, he had set up a private medical institute to treat rabies, do scientific research, and train young scientists and doctors in laboratory work.

Edison and Eiffel

In spite of all the honors heaped on Edison, and the pleasure he took in meeting people such as Louis Pasteur, the highlight of Paris for him was the Eiffel Tower. Finally, during his last week in Paris, he met its builder. When the French prime minister held yet another banquet to honor Edison, he invited Gustave Eiffel, who had just returned to Paris.

"I think Eiffel is the nicest fellow I have met since I came to France," Edison later told Robert Sherard. "He is so simple and modest." Like everyone else in Paris, Eiffel wanted to celebrate Edison and invited him to lunch on the tower. Edison was delighted. The lunch would take place on September 10.

That morning was cool and breezy. Larger-than-usual crowds lined up at the foot of the tower. Gustave Eiffel, who had welcomed princes and politicians of every rank there, waited eagerly for the man he viewed as his most important visitor yet, the great American inventor.

Eiffel had gathered sixty of his engineering colleagues for a formal lunch in Edison's honor at one of the cafés on the first platform. Eiffel's older sister, his daughter, and his son-in-law were also present. The engineers and ladies settled in for a pleasant meal of many courses. The golden afternoon glided past.

After a while, the dessert plates were cleared away. Eiffel rose to toast Edison, whom he called "[o]ur dear and illustrious master." Edison, in turn, rose and toasted Eiffel and his "beautiful work." And so, Thomas Edison, who was quite deaf and spoke no French, and Gustave Eiffel, who spoke only a little English, celebrated their meeting in the best French way: by drinking champagne on the world's tallest structure.

As the domes and church spires of Paris glowed in the afternoon light, the seventy-five guests ascended to Eiffel's private apartment for coffee and brandy. In the background was the artist A. A. Anderson. He was best known for his oil portraits and had already made one of Edison. Now Eiffel had asked him to capture Edison as best he could in a sculpture.

Edison enjoyed himself immensely on this day, but he did so quietly because of his deafness and his inability to speak French. Later, journalist Sherard told Eiffel how much Edison had admired him and his tower. Eiffel said, "I am glad to hear it, for when Edison lunched with me . . . he hardly spoke, and I should have liked to hear his opinion."

Sherard could not resist telling Eiffel something else that Edison had said: that New York would build a tower twice as tall as Eiffel's. Eiffel said very quietly, "[N]ous verrons cela." (We'll see about that.)

The next day, the Edisons left for Germany. As the inventor left Paris, he enchanted the French by announcing a gift of $2,000 to help the poor of Paris. During the next two weeks, Edison enjoyed a triumphant tour through Germany. He and Mina then took a ferry to England, where he kept his promise to stay with Sir John Pender at his estate.

The Eiffel Tower and
the 1889 World's Fair
grounds.

On the night of September 26, Thomas and Mina Edison slipped quietly back across the English Channel for a last night in Paris. Thomas then received a note from Minister Whitelaw Reid inviting him to come that evening to the minister's home. It included the mysterious words "I've got something for you."

When Edison arrived, he found many guests who had just finished dinner and were enjoying cigars. Reid rose and announced that French president Sadi Carnot had sent a gift for Edison. He handed Edison a large plush case. Edison bowed and tucked it under his arm.

"Hold on there," said Reid. "Let's see what you've got there." Edison reluctantly opened the box. Inside was a broad red sash with a medal hanging from it. The French had raised Edison to the rank of commander of the Legion of Honor, the highest rank a foreigner could hold. Edison blushed with embarrassment and said, "I never in the world could wear it."

After a final carriage ride through the night streets of Paris, with the colored lights of the Eiffel Tower blazing across the river, Edison returned to the rooms where he and his wife were staying and showed the medal to Mina. She danced around the room in glee and then hung the sash around her husband's neck, arranging the medal just so. It was the final, fitting touch to their visit to France. The next day, they set sail for New York on a French ocean liner with the perfect name: *La Champagne.*

CHAPTER TWELVE
LAST DAYS

AS THE SUMMER OF 1889 DREW TO A CLOSE, SO did the wonderful Paris Universal Exposition. The last day of October would be the end of the fair. Suddenly, people who had not yet been to the fair headed toward Paris. And Parisians who *had* been, knowing that it would soon be over, found every excuse to make return visits.

One who returned was Edmond de Goncourt. As evening fell on a day in mid-October, he paid a visit to the Forestry Pavilion. The fading light had an enchanting effect. "For me," he wrote, "it was truly like entering into a magic palace, built by woodland fairies, its towering columns fashioned from the mammoth trunks of ancient

287

Rosa Bonheur poses with Rocky Bear, William Cody, her art dealers, Red Shirt, and an unknown man.

trees, each of the most subtle colors of the wings of night-flying moths."

Fair attendance was high during those final weeks. On Sunday, October 6, such huge crowds flowed happily through the gates that by the end of the day, a new daily record had been set: 307,000 people had paid to enter.

As the days ticked by, a campaign arose for the fair to remain open a bit longer. Finally, on October 12, the fair commissioners agreed to extend the fair an extra six days, ending it exactly six months after it had opened. "We have the Exposition till November 6!" one gleeful journalist exclaimed. "It's the big news of the week. Six extra days of this fairyland."

By that time, the final weeks of the fair had already seen new successes and surprises, including an unexpected friendship for Buffalo Bill Cody.

The Wild West Gets an Artist

September 5 was a cold day in Paris, with hints of autumn. It was also the day Buffalo Bill entertained one more famous person. This time it was Rosa Bonheur, a sixty-seven-year-old French artist.

Rosa Bonheur at her easel, painting Buffalo Bill.

Bonheur was well known in England and the United States for her paintings of animals, which had made her rich. One of them, *The Horse Fair*, was a gift from American millionaire Cornelius Vanderbilt to the Metropolitan Museum of Art in New York. Bonheur was also the first woman to have been made a chevalier in the Legion of Honor. The empress of France had presented her with the red ribbon in 1865.

Short, stout, and white-haired, wearing a fur-trimmed coat over her full skirt and smart boots on her tiny feet, Bonheur visited the Wild West show with her American and French art dealers. Buffalo Bill escorted her and the dealers over the grounds. Bonheur silently absorbed the sights. She looked in wonder at the grazing buffalo, at the campfires burning before the tents and teepees, and at the Indians ambling about. Cody invited his guests to join him in his tent for a private lunch with Chiefs Red Shirt and Rocky Bear. Afterward, a photograph was taken as a remembrance for Bonheur of "a memory I really relish."

That first visit to the Wild West camp was the beginning of a friendship with Buffalo Bill. It was also the start of a new role for Rosa Bonheur. She became the unofficial artist-in-residence at the camp. Many mornings that September, she left her carriage and strolled about until she found an Indian scene that suited her eye. By late September she was a regular sight in the camp. Among other projects, she completed a small portrait of Buffalo Bill cantering along on his beloved white horse, Tucker, with the horse's long, full white tail swishing behind. The painting would later have a prominent place in Cody's Nebraska home.

Bonheur's greatest fascination, though, was with the Indians. She developed what she called "a real passion for this unfortunate race," saying, "[I]t's utterly deplorable that they're doomed to extinction by white usurpers." She painted a double portrait of Red Shirt and Rocky Bear riding solemnly through a scrubby countryside. Other Wild West Indians also posed for Bonheur. The sketches she made of them would inspire seventeen paintings over the next few years.

Later Bonheur said, "Observing [the Indians] at close range really refreshed my sad old mind. I was free to work among [them], drawing and painting them with their horses, weapons, camps, and animals. . . . Buffalo Bill was extremely good to me."

A WOMAN IN PANTS

FOR YEARS, ROSA BONHEUR WAS AS FAMOUS for the way she dressed as for her paintings of powerful and noble animals. In the 1850s she had become one of the few women in France to have an official permit to dress in men's clothes. The permit, which had to be renewed every six months, allowed her to wear pants, as long as she did not do so at balls, shows, and certain other public meeting places.

Bonheur had argued that she needed to wear men's clothing as a disguise. No respectable woman would go alone into places such as slaughterhouses or horse and cattle fairs, where she needed to sketch and paint.

One view from the Eiffel Tower's first-floor promenade.

    Now the artist no longer worked in such places, but at home she still favored a more elegant version of men's clothing. Her typical outfit was loose velvet trousers, an embroidered peasant smock with amethyst buttons on the collar, and leather boots. Knowing that occasional visitors would be shocked by the sight of a woman in pants, Bonheur always kept a skirt handy for quick changes.

Buffalo Bill Returns the Visit

Rosa Bonheur rarely invited people to visit her at home, but she made an exception for Buffalo Bill. She asked him to come see her studio and her animals.

Bonheur lived in a picturesque country house on the edge of a forest south of Paris. The mansion's carriage house served as her art studio. Her menagerie of animals included dogs, horses, sheep, cows, mountain goats, an eagle and other birds, a tame stag, and a pet lioness named Fatima. Cody's arrival set off "the barking of numerous dogs, the hounds and bassets in chorus, the grand Saint Bernard in slow measure, like the bass drum in an orchestra." Somewhere a parrot squawked.

Among Bonheur's animals at the time were a pair of American mustangs, housed in a meadow that she owned. She had received them as gifts from admirers in the American West. One of the horses, Apache, was too wild to be tamed. Bonheur told Cody that if his cowboys could catch the mustangs, Cody could keep them. He gladly accepted the offer.

A few days later, two cowboys showed up, and Bonheur and her neighbors lined the meadow fence to watch the show. The first cowboy lassoed Apache on his second try and soon tied his legs and slipped a halter onto him. Speaking softly to the struggling horse, the cowboy eased on a blanket and saddle, then mounted the mustang. Apache took off, bucking wildly.

The French expected the cowboy to be thrown off as Apache hurled himself ferociously about the meadow. Instead, the cowboy calmly rode Apache round and round until slowly the mustang calmed. The second cowboy repeated the feat with the other mustang. Before long, to the amazement of the locals, the two Americans rode the animals down the country road to a train station and into a stable car. Rosa Bonheur, as astonished as her neighbors, congratulated them.

Bonheur later told the Wyoming man who had given Apache to her that the horse had been too wild for her. "I thought I was doing the right thing by turning him over to Buffalo Bill," she said. "Those fellows really know how to handle ornery beasts without hurting them. It's a real pleasure to watch them work. After one of them lassoed your little horse, he calmed him down so well that he was able to go up and stroke his head. That's a task I never could have given to a French groom."

The Beginning of the End

On September 30, the journalists and typesetters of the tower edition of *Le Figaro* put together the final issue of their paper. "Tomorrow begins the last month of the Exposition," wrote the editor in his farewell column.

He continued:

> *The days will become much shorter, the mornings above all, while the evenings will be much cooler; soon enough the foreigners will be thinking of leaving us. . . . It seems to us, also, that our task is largely complete. . . . Our little newspaper will appear no more; but our pavilion remains open to friends and all visitors to the tower. Friends will find there, as in the past, shelter when it rains . . . and a register ready for their signatures; ascensionnistes [people who went up the tower] can still receive a certificate of ascension.*

Other Parisians shared the feeling of wistful farewell to the fair combined with an awareness of how it had changed their city. A journalist who had scorned the Eiffel Tower early on had changed his mind about it. Through the September fogs, he wrote, he looked expectantly for the light at the top of the tower.

"It has become the true crown of Paris," he wrote, "and for five long months already it has shone, shone, shone, seen by all, attracting so many people, like a lighthouse . . . one could say that this little luminous crown is the ray that shines above all else, at this moment, illuminating up there something which we dearly love, a flag that appears little seen from below, but is huge up close, waving in the wind, the beautiful French tricoleur." (The French flag is called the tricolor because it has three colors: blue, white, and red.)

Edison Looks Back and Ahead

The steamship *La Champagne*, with the Edisons on board, entered New York Harbor on October 6, the same day that crowds to the Paris fair set the all-time attendance record. The ship was greeted by a smaller boat carrying Edison Company officials, who had brought a band to welcome their chief with music. They hailed the couple with happy yells of "Count and Countess Edison!"

That evening, Edison held court for reporters in his New Jersey home. "I went over to see the Exposition," he said. "It was a big show. Couldn't begin to see all of it. Acres and acres of things to look at." When asked what kind of showing the United States had made at the fair, Edison was blunt: "Very poor. Even the little South American republics beat us hollow."

He proudly told of his many honors, but reassured the *New York Times*, "I am just as much of an American as ever. . . . They tried their best to spoil me, but my head is not a jot larger than it was, and this week you will see me back in harness as before."

Once again Edison sang the praises of the Eiffel Tower, calling it "a wonderful thing." He could not resist adding patriotically that it had taken American know-how to design and make the elevators that rose up the tower's curved legs. Edison also spoke optimistically about the prospects of a world's fair in the United States in a few years. New York City, he thought, was the natural spot for it. Of course, the Americans would build a tower fifteen hundred or two thousand feet tall to outshine Eiffel's creation.

The *New York Times* reported that Edison said
that such a feat "is not an engineering problem."

The Butterfly Stings Again

While the Universal Exposition was winding
down in Paris, artist James McNeill Whistler
and his wife had finally left London. They
had not gone to Paris, however. Instead, their
destination was Amsterdam, in the Netherlands,
where Whistler had a few pieces in an art show.

One rainy afternoon a writer for the *Herald*
dropped in to see the Whistlers at their hotel.
As they chatted over wine and walnuts, the
journalist was delighted to discover that the ever-
argumentative Whistler was renewing his feud
with General Hawkins, who had been in charge
of the American art exhibit at the Paris fair.

Whistler talked about why he had taken his art
to the British exhibit instead of leaving it with the
other American works. "I did not mind the fact that
my sketches were criticized," he said, "but it was
the discourteous manner in which it was done."

Hawkins had spent the summer being abused
by one complaining artist after another. He had
had enough. After reading the interview with

Whistler, Hawkins struck back in the *Herald* the next day. "I have never in my life written a line to Mr. Whistler. What he did receive was a circular with my name printed at the bottom. . . . It is a little singular that among about one hundred and fifty artists who received this circular, Mr. Whistler should have been the only one to discover its latent discourtesy." Hawkins added that if Whistler had had "a more even temper and a little more commonsense," he would have been able to show five or six works in the American exhibit, instead of the three he showed with the British.

Various other artists seized the opportunity to hurl a few more of their own insults and grievances at Hawkins in the *Herald*. Again, Hawkins replied, writing, "I never allow myself to be drawn into mud-slinging contests. . . . There are two sides to this story, and so far, only one has been told—the story of the sour-grapes contingent."

Of course, Whistler *would* have the last word. From Amsterdam he wrote, "It is a sad shock to me to find that the Good General speaks of me without affection. . . . The truth is, and always has been, that . . . he knows no more about art than the fly that crawls wearily over some of the panoramas in our department."

Artists' Misfortunes

The winding down of the Universal Exposition brought no joy to artist Paul Gauguin. He had failed to make any impression at all during the fair. "Nothing either in the daily papers or in the so-called art periodicals," he said sadly. "Isn't that fine?"

It had been a triumph for Gauguin to be able to hang his work on the walls of Volpini's café at the fair. But although thousands of people had eaten there over the summer, not one of Gauguin's paintings had been sold. In September the discouraged artist went to a place in the country where he could live cheaply while he looked for some kind of job in France's colonies. Above all, Gauguin yearned for the tropics.

Vincent van Gogh, Gauguin's fellow artist, had had a wrenching summer of illness. But by August he was painting feverishly again. In September he wrote to his brother, Theo, "I am working like one actually possessed. . . . And I think that this will help cure me. . . . How can I tell, but I think I have one or two canvases going that are not so bad."

Theo was deeply impressed with his brother's latest paintings. He especially admired two of them: *The Irises* and *Starry Night*. Theo had submitted these works to a Paris art show that was open to all. After that, an artists' group had invited Vincent to show work at its yearly show in Belgium, which was quite an honor. And an artist and writer had singled Vincent van Gogh out for highest praise in an article, saying, "[H]is name is destined to go down in the succeeding generations. There will be more in time to say about this remarkable hero—a Dutchman."

Final Moments

For the many people who exhibited products, inventions, and other goods at the fair, it had been a long summer. They were waiting for the awarding of prizes in various categories. Finally, the exhibition jury published its list of winners on September 29.

It was not a short list. There was a total of 33,000 winners in every possible category. Still, those who had been passed over did not take it well. An American reporter strolling the aisles of the fair noted that some exhibitors had put signs on their stalls "worded in more or less bitter language," or were displaying their goods upside down. Although the fair might be almost over, its administrators did not tolerate such behavior. They threatened legal action against exhibitors who did not follow the rules.

November rolled in wet and cold, but still crowds swarmed the fair in its last week. On the final Sunday, torrents of rain pummeled the sightseers as well as the somewhat bedraggled fairgrounds, which were full of gaps where exhibitors had left. Yet neither the foul weather nor the absent exhibits and taken-apart cafés could dampen the holiday mood.

Tuesday, the fair's second-to-last day, dawned rainy, wet, and miserable. Clouds blotted out the top of the Eiffel Tower. And yet more people flocked to the fair for a last look. On Wednesday, the rain cleared for the final day. Festive crowds poured in to enjoy the closing ceremonies. When darkness fell, a full moon rose high in the sky. The mood was magical.

At nine o'clock, all eyes turned to the Eiffel Tower. Thousands of fireworks transformed the world's largest structure into red fire. The fountains at its base were lighted green, violet, and red. Thousands of Chinese lanterns hung from trees and bushes.

High up in the tower, Gustave Eiffel had gathered fifty friends at his apartment to mark this last evening of the great Paris Universal Exposition of 1889. William Hammer of the Edison Company arrived with a gift: a wax cylinder from Thomas Edison. Eiffel opened his Edison phonograph and played the cylinder. The lovely sound of opera music floated on the air, followed by the voice of Edison himself, thanking Eiffel for his time on the tower.

Gustave Eiffel had tasted a success such as few men had known. He was thoroughly savoring it.

And so the Universal Exposition came to an end. It was a phenomenal achievement. The French could not help but glory in their triumph. Visitors both French and foreign had spent an estimated $324 million at the fair. One French paper boasted, "The Exhibition has brought to France much foreign money, but, what is better, is the change that has taken place in the opinions of foreigners with respect to France." The nation's young republic had not just shown its industrial power to the world. It had organized and operated one of the biggest public events in history.

The nocturnal Eiffel Tower ablaze with light.

CHAPTER THIRTEEN

AFTER THE FAIR

THE 1889 WORLD'S FAIR IN PARIS WAS "THE most successful affair of this kind that has ever been organized," said the *Washington Post*, an American newspaper, after the fair was over. "Not only has this great show reflected great credit on those who conceived it and carried it out, pouring millions into the pockets of thrifty Frenchmen, but it has put the French republic on a more secure foundation . . . and has driven its enemies into exile." And yet the *Post* predicted that the world's fair of 1893, the Columbian Exposition, which would be held in the American city of Chicago, would be bigger and better.

Gustave Eiffel.

The Paris fair had brought together an extraordinary group of people: artists, Wild Westerners, a colorful newspaper publisher, an ambitious inventor, and above all the master engineer who had built the Eiffel Tower. In the years that followed the fair, some of them found glory, while others found difficulty and even tragedy. And one of them, the man who had risen to the top of the world by creating the tower, fell farthest of all, only to rise again.

Eiffel's Fall

On January 11, 1893, Gustave Eiffel found himself once again in the public eye. This time he was not in his familiar role of heroic engineer atop his marvelous tower of iron. Instead, he was the defendant in a criminal case.

In a packed courtroom, Eiffel was being grilled along with four officers of the bankrupt Panama Canal Company. The five men were accused of fraud against the now-ruined people who had bought shares in the company.

In the hush of the courtroom, Eiffel reluctantly admitted that he had made a $6.6 million profit on his contract to build the canal locks for $13.8 million. The spectators gasped.

Angry murmurs arose from the crowd. Eiffel was seen to shudder.

The Paris world's fair had been such a success that it had taken some time for French outrage over the collapse of the Panama Canal Company to boil over. Americans, however, had long had doubts about the venture. As early as 1888, the *New York Times* had reported that it was "almost funny" that anyone still believed in the Panama Canal scheme. The paper reported that a clerk had borrowed a sizable sum of money to buy shares in the Canal Company, convinced that it would be "just so much treasured gold for his children."

That clerk was only one of the many French investors who wanted to know how almost $300 million of their money had disappeared into a tropical swamp. The Panama Affair, as it was called, became one of the great scandals of modern French history. Not only had the company wasted vast sums on a sea-level canal that could not work, but it had also paid millions in bribes to politicians and members of the French press to support its shaky share offerings. This had encouraged French families to throw their money into the company.

One canal promoter fled to England. Another apparently killed himself. That left Eiffel and four others to face justice in the courtroom, where the angry audience enjoyed their comeuppance. Eiffel and the others sat stunned when the judge pronounced them guilty, one by one. Eiffel was sentenced to a $4,000 fine and two years in jail.

Eiffel's tower had made him world-famous, one of the most admired men in France, and richer than ever. But the same public that had praised his triumph now assumed he must in fact be a liar and scoundrel. He had made far too much money on the canal venture when, all around, tens of thousands of people had lost their small savings. One old silk maker spoke for them when he described his helpless fury at the loss of the money he had saved through half a century of hard work: "I am a man of order, but I say strongly that if a chance presents itself, I will secure justice myself." Another ruined shareholder threatened in a note to Eiffel, "Your house will be blown up by dynamite."

In June, Eiffel presented himself to serve his prison sentence. He walked through the grim corridors of France's most famous dungeon, where Queen Marie Antoinette had spent the final weeks before her beheading. Then he came to the cell where he would pass the next two years: a small, stone-walled room furnished with a bed, a table, and a chair. From a high barred window, Eiffel could see only the barges passing on the Seine.

One week later, he and another Panama Canal prisoner were brought out to a waiting room. There Eiffel saw his lawyers and several family members. They cried out joyfully that a higher court had just undone his guilty verdict. There would be no new charges. Eiffel was a free man. Clutching his son, he began to weep.

The Legion of Honor, which had given its award to Eiffel, also investigated the matter. It found that although Eiffel had earned a gigantic profit, he had built the locks as agreed until he was ordered to stop. He had no position in the Panama Canal Company and had played no part in the vast network of bribes. The Legion found nothing wrong in Eiffel's behavior.

Still, Eiffel's reputation was blackened. He removed his name from his own company and took no part in any new big engineering projects. A decade later, a journalist wrote that many people still held very bitter feelings toward Eiffel. They could not look at his tower without remembering that first guilty verdict in the Panama Affair. The journalist added, however, that he believed Eiffel to be a straightforward, energetic, and honest man of business.

The Artists

For the brothers Theo and Vincent van Gogh, the years following the fair held triumph and tragedy alike. Vincent's paintings received some praise. One of them even sold. But Vincent had been suffering from seizures. After a brief visit to Theo in Paris, he moved to a village that was popular with painters. A doctor there agreed to take him as a patient. Soon Vincent was spending long hours painting in the open air.

At the same time, though, Theo's health went downhill. Then he received an urgent summons from Vincent's doctor. He arrived in the village to find Vincent in bed, wrapped in bloody bandages. The day before, he had shot himself in the stomach. Theo wrote to his wife, "You could not imagine there was so much sorrow in life." Before long, Vincent died in Theo's arms.

Paul Gauguin, Vincent's fellow artist and

former roommate, wrote in a letter, "Sad though his death may be, I am not very grieved, for I knew it was coming and I knew how this poor fellow suffered in his struggles with madness." Theo soon showed signs of insanity as well. He promised Gauguin that he would provide money to send the artist to the tropics, which Gauguin urgently desired. Gauguin was angry and disappointed when he learned that Theo van Gogh was now as mad as his dead brother. Theo died in 1891 at the age of thirty-three.

Gauguin, meanwhile, devoted all his energy to one goal. He wanted to go to Tahiti, in the South Pacific. He felt his art would flourish there. A month after Theo's death, Gauguin held a successful sale of his art. Shortly afterward, he set sail for the South Pacific.

Gauguin returned from Tahiti to France in 1893, hoping for the fame and success that had escaped him at the 1889 world's fair. After only modest success and a period of street brawls, lost paintings, and a turbulent personal life, Gauguin went back to the South Pacific in 1895. Although he became the toast of artistic Paris after a show of his Tahitian paintings, he was isolated and ill in the South Pacific. In 1903 he was found dead in his squalid house on the tiny island of Hiva Oa.

As for American artist James McNeill Whistler, he and his wife moved to Paris three years after the fair. Whistler wrote to a friend that he had come to a "land of light and joy where honors are heaped upon me." The government of France had honored him by making him a member of the Legion of Honor. It had also bought one of his paintings, *Arrangement in Grey and Black, No. 1: Portrait of the Artist's Mother*. This work, now usually called *Whistler's Mother*, was hung in the Louvre, the great art museum in Paris. Whistler finally had the official praise he had long wanted.

Ever the social butterfly, Whistler often entertained visitors at his Paris home. He had become a famous American in Paris. And to his glee, for the first time in his career he sold his work for big prices. He still enjoyed arguments and insults, however. The French painter Edgar Degas wondered why Whistler was so fond of verbal sparring, saying, "He should paint with his tongue; then he might be a genius."

Whistler's charmed Paris period did not last long. He returned to England to seek

medical care for his wife, who died of cancer
in 1896. After her death, Whistler tried living
in Paris again, but by 1899 he had drifted back
to London. His artistic drive and ambition
had faded, and he was often ill. He died of
pneumonia in 1903, just two months after
Gauguin died halfway around the world.

Indian Troubles

Building on his huge success in Paris, Buffalo Bill
Cody took the Wild West show on a tour through
the cities of southern Europe. In the Spanish city
of Barcelona an epidemic of influenza raged, and
half the show's company got sick. Among the
ill were Oakley and narrator Frank Richmond.
Oakley recovered, but Richmond died.

Cody fled with the performers and animals
to Naples, Italy. There, Oakley's health improved
while she enjoyed the warm sunshine and the
sights. She went up the volcano Mount Vesuvius
and said, "Standing on the shaking top of
Vesuvius, I had the desire to look down into the
crater though the lava was falling thick about me."

Outbreaks of disease had already killed several
of the show's Indians in Marseilles, France.
In Naples the company lost two more Indians.

THE NEXT BIGGEST THING?

CHICAGO HAD WON THE RIGHT TO HOST A
world's fair that would be held in 1893 and called
the Columbian Exposition. Of course, it needed
an astounding structure to serve as a centerpiece,
the way the Eiffel Tower had served the 1889 fair.
Competition to build something greater than the
Eiffel Tower began to heat up.

Before being swallowed up by the Panama Canal
scandal, Eiffel himself had offered to build a taller
version of his Paris monument in Chicago. American
engineers were outraged that the Frenchman should
try to claim an American prize. Their own proposals,
however, were strange and impractical.

One company envisioned a tower nearly nine
times the height of the Eiffel Tower. Rails would lead
from the top of the tower to such cities as New York

Chicago World's Fair, 1893.

and Boston. Visitors to the fair who were daring enough to ride elevators to the top of the Chicago tower could then glide downhill all the way home.

Even stranger was a proposal for a four-thousand-foot tower with a two-thousand-foot rubber cable attached to it. Passengers would ride in a car attached to the cable, which "would be shoved off a platform and fall without restraint to the end of the cable." The designer recommended that the ground around the tower be covered with eight feet of feather bedding, just in case. A third proposal was for a log cabin tower made of giant trees.

The men in charge of the Chicago fair were getting worried. Where was the American engineering marvel that would equal the Eiffel Tower, or surpass it?

Finally, they accepted a proposal from a man named George Washington Ferris. It was for a gigantic revolving wheel with passenger cars that could carry more than two thousand people at a time to a height of three hundred feet, slightly higher than the crown of the Statue of Liberty (but less than a third the height of the Eiffel Tower).

This Ferris wheel never came close to rivaling the elegance and fame of the Eiffel Tower. Still, it was something new, and it had its own enchantments. It glittered in the night sky. More than a million visitors to the Chicago fair paid to ride it—fewer than half the number that had paid to go up the Eiffel Tower.

Still, the show went on as the Wild West worked its way north through Italy. The Italian tour ended with a day of pleasure in Venice, the city of canals. Buffalo Bill and all the cowboys and Indians, with the chiefs in full ceremonial headdress, took a lazy trip up and down the city's main canal in its famous gondolas, boats pushed along with poles. The troupe then moved north into central Europe.

The Wild West shows were sold out, and some of the troupe's members received lavish gifts—Annie Oakley especially treasured a diamond bracelet given to her by the ruler of Bavaria, in what is now southern Germany. But some of the Indians had had enough. Red Shirt and his family had sailed home after Barcelona. Other small groups of Indians followed during the summer of 1890.

Five Sioux from the show landed in New York in June. One of the men was Kills Plenty, whose right arm had been crushed when a horse fell on him in Germany. He died of blood poisoning within days of landing in New York. The press paid attention to this death—and to other Wild West Indians who soon arrived from Europe. Homesick and unhappy, these former members of the show were happy to tell reporters about their discontents.

The U.S. Interior Department's Office of Indian Affairs had wanted for a long time to end performances by Indians that promoted "savagery" and the old Indian way of life. Officials there closely followed the news about the Wild West show's Indian woes.

That fall, two more Wild West Indians died in Germany. The Office of Indian Affairs announced that it was making a formal investigation. In addition, it would issue no further work permits for Indians. The managers of the Wild West show were genuinely alarmed. Without the Sioux, there would be no show. Major Burke, one of the managers, sailed for New York with the remaining thirty-eight Indians, to prove that all of them were in good health and to fight the Office of Indian Affairs' new ruling.

In Washington, Burke and some of the Indians testified at the Indian Office. Black Heart explained that the Indian performers were treated exactly the same as the whites. Rocky Bear showed a purse filled with gold coins, proof that the Indians were earning money. They all

Buffalo Bill and Indians
taking a gondola ride in
Venice, spring 1890.

said that they hoped to return to the show in Europe. In November, Cody himself arrived in New York to further challenge the Indian Office. But while Cody was brooding about how to get his Indian performers back, he received a telegram summoning him on a secret mission.

A Mission to Sitting Bull

The telegram Cody received was from General Nelson Miles, famous for his military actions against the Indians. His forces had captured the chief Geronimo. Now Miles called on Buffalo Bill Cody to return to his old role as an Indian scout for the government.

It was a grim moment in the history of the Sioux. A recent treaty had opened eleven million acres of Sioux land to white miners and settlers. The official plan was for the Sioux, a people who had always wandered freely across their lands, to settle down as farmers. Three years of drought had undermined that plan. Even as crops withered, the government cut its rations of food to the Standing Rock and Pine Ridge reservations. Indians were starving and falling ill.

At this desperate time, Chief Sitting Bull had joined tribes across the plains in embracing the

Ghost Dance movement. Ghost Dances were rituals that some Indians believed would call up a new Indian savior who would do away with white people and their civilization, restoring the traditional Indian world and way of life. Ghost Dancing was seen as a first step toward war.

Miles wanted Cody to undertake a secret mission to urge peace on Sitting Bull. The old chief had toured with the Wild West show in its first season, and he still rode a gray horse that Cody had given him. Yet Cody did not seem hopeful about his mission. While on his way west, he told a reporter in Chicago, "Of all the bad Indians, Sitting Bull is the worst. . . . He is a dangerous Indian and his conduct now portends trouble."

Cody realized that if there were an Indian war, he would be in a strange position. "I don't yet know whether I shall fight them or not," he told another journalist. "It might not look exactly right for me to do so, for I have made a fortune out of them, but if they get to shedding innocent blood[,] I may, if I can be of any service, go up there."

Days later Cody was on his way to Sitting Bull's camp, traveling by a mule-drawn wagon through bitter winter weather, when a messenger caught up with him and handed him another telegram. President Benjamin Harrison had called off Cody's mission at the request of the government official in charge of the Standing Rock reservation. Annoyed but dutiful, Cody turned around. He would go to his home in Nebraska instead of meeting with Sitting Bull.

Two weeks later, the U.S. Indian Police raided Sitting Bull's cabin, planning to arrest him. Instead, the old chief was killed, along with seven of his warriors. U.S. troops poured into the region in case of an Indian uprising. Major Burke had brought the Wild West Indians home to their Pine Ridge reservation, where they enlisted in the Indian Police, hoping this would persuade the U.S. government to give them work permits in time for the show's spring tour in Europe. Meanwhile, Sioux warriors camped in the surrounding plains and valleys, and American troops slowly encircled them. It was the largest gathering of U.S. Army troops since the Civil War.

On December 29, 1890, a band of Sioux and their families were supposed to surrender to soldiers at Wounded Knee Creek. A scuffle between a soldier and an Indian turned into a massacre. Almost two hundred Indians were killed. Many were women and children who had been trying to flee. General Miles began arresting Ghost Dance leaders in the hope of preventing more violence.

A week later, Buffalo Bill rode into the tense atmosphere of Pine Ridge. The governor of Nebraska had sent him to help General Miles. Major Burke wrote articles for the newspaper under Cody's name, with such thrilling statements as "[T]he smoldering spark is visible that may precipitate a terrible conflict any time in the next few days." Soon afterward, the outgunned Ghost Dancers and their followers surrendered to Miles.

Cody and his Wild West Indians had not had to fight, yet Cody's reputation as a fighter had been boosted by the whole affair. Better yet, political pressure in favor of Cody forced the Office of Indian Affairs to give work permits not only to twenty-three Ghost Dance prisoners who would be sent to Europe with Cody, but also to seventy-five more Sioux who wanted to join the show. On April 1, 1891, Burke hustled the Indians onto a steamship before the Office of Indian Affairs could change its mind.

A Bigger, Bolder Show

Back in Europe, Nate Salsbury had not known whether the Indians would be allowed to return to the show. To make up for their absence, he had hired colorful horsemen from Russia, Argentina, and elsewhere. When Burke and his Indians returned, the familiar Wild West show became interwoven with astounding feats of foreign horsemanship. Bearded Cossacks from southern Russia, equipped with curved swords and long rifles, raced into the arena and performed acrobatics such as standing on their heads atop their galloping steeds. Gauchos from the plains of Argentina hurled their bolas (iron balls on rawhide thongs) across the arena with deadly accuracy. The new show was billed as "Buffalo Bill's Wild West and Congress of Rough Riders of the World." It was a huge success and set the pattern for the Wild West show for the next ten years.

The show earned money year after year, but Cody always teetered on the edge of financial ruin. In 1915 he spent a long, difficult season working for another showman after he failed to repay a loan. The following year, once again his own boss, he toured from spring to November. A

The poster for the show in the 1890s.

reporter who saw him after the tour recalled that "[T]he old scout was in pajamas and slippers . . . his hand out in a last farewell. . . . It was the last time. I knew it; he knew it; we all knew it. But on the surface not a sign." In January 1917, Cody died at his sister's house, surrounded by his family.

The American nation mourned its Wild West hero. Cowboys, Indians, and grizzled old scouts were among the twenty-five thousand people who passed through the Colorado State Capitol while his body rested there before burial. Buffalo Bill had risen to fame by bringing together the sights and sounds of the frontier with the brilliant lights and colorful publicity of a modern entertainment. To Americans, he represented an old world that was vanishing and the promise of the new one that was dawning.

Annie Oakley did not make it to Buffalo Bill's funeral, but she wrote, "William F. Cody was the kindest hearted, simplest, most loyal man I ever knew." She and Frank Butler had settled into a good life working at two fashionable resorts in Florida and North Carolina. They returned in 1926 to home and family in Ohio, where Oakley died that year at the age of sixty-six.

The Inventor

During the golden days of the 1889 Paris world's fair, Thomas Edison had often bragged that Americans were sure to build a tower twice as tall as Eiffel's. But once he was back in his laboratory in New Jersey, Edison had problems.

His biggest backer on Wall Street was financier J. P. Morgan. Unknown to Edison, Morgan had been working to sell Edison's electric company out from under him. By 1892, without so much as a word to the great inventor, Morgan merged Edison Electric into a new company he named General Electric.

To escape his business troubles, Edison went to a wild stretch of New Jersey to work on a giant ore-crushing machine that would smash rock into powder. The idea was that a super-powerful magnet would then pull valuable iron ore out of the powder. Edison worked happily on this project, convinced he was on the brink of a huge success. From time to time, though, he pulled himself away from his bleak testing area (and from the project that would turn out to be the biggest waste of time and resources in his career) to work on other inventions in his lab.

BUFFALO BILL AND ANNIE OAKLEY IN CHICAGO

THE DIRECTORS OF THE 1893 CHICAGO Columbian Exposition had turned down Buffalo Bill's bid for a spot inside the fairgrounds. So the show got hold of fourteen acres right across from the main entrance to the fair and built its arena and campground there. One of the main attractions was Sitting Bull's bullet-ridden cabin. Although the Paris fair would always be the high point of Cody's professional life, he is thought to have made a million dollars in profits at the Chicago fair.

Annie Oakley's success in Europe had increased her fame at home. She was a huge star at the Chicago fair. Like Buffalo Bill, she was an

Chicago World's Fair, 1893.

example of the American Dream: a person from a humble beginning who had achieved the heights of success by hard work and talent.

Oakley was also a representative of the spunky modern woman. She was self-reliant and as good as a man (or better) at shooting. She had begun riding a bicycle, which added to her image as up-to-the-minute. She always encouraged women to master outdoor pursuits and taught gun skills to thousands of them over the years. At the same time, in her home life Oakley remained the happily married Mrs. Butler who liked nothing better than being out in nature. A Chicago reporter wrote, "There is not a nicer wife or woman in the land than Annie Oakley."

He and his assistants were continually improving the phonograph to make it a commercial success. Edison was also developing the Kinetoscope, a primitive motion-picture machine that played a short scene for a nickel.

In 1893, Edison wrote about this motion-picture device that he was "very doubtful if there is any commercial feature in it." The next year, he was proven utterly wrong. The first small Kinetoscope parlor, with five machines, opened in New York City. Customers got to see a ninety-second scene of prizefighting. As word spread about moving pictures, customers mobbed the street. They were so eager that police had to control the lines of people waiting to enter. Motion pictures clearly had a future.

Edison quickly built a film studio in West Orange, where his lab was located. His men used it to churn out frantically active short films for the booming Kinetoscope market. A steady stream of people came to the studio to be recorded. Among them were boxers, dancers, strongmen, and people who performed comic skits. It was in Edison's West Orange film studio that two American stars of the 1889 world's fair, Thomas Edison and Buffalo Bill, were reunited.

Thomas Edison and
his new, improved
phonograph.

Buffalo Bill's touring company was finishing a run in New York when he led fifteen of the Wild West Indians to West Orange to act out famous frontier scenes for the camera. Annie Oakley had her turn later, and Edison was delighted to see how the camera captured the way her guns smoked and glass balls shattered during her sharpshooting act. Little did Buffalo Bill Cody imagine that the motion pictures that began in that little New Jersey studio would slowly lure away the audience for the live spectacles that had made him so much money.

In the coming years, Edison had to admit that his ore-crushing machine was a hopeless failure. He was rich enough not to be too concerned about it, though. Sales of phonographs and the cylinders to play on them skyrocketed. So did the motion picture business. By 1909, eight thousand theaters offered "movies." These films were typically fourteen minutes long and featured wrecked trains, ladies rescued from villains, and terrible calamities. Edison cheerfully told a friend that his inventions were making "a great amount of money."

In 1911, Edison returned to Paris for the first time in twenty-two years, on a family vacation.

He boasted to reporters about his new "talking pictures." One subject he did *not* talk about was the Eiffel Tower and why America had not yet built something taller and better.

The Edison family spent two busy months driving around Switzerland, Germany, and France. Many people feared that Europe was headed toward war. When Edison was asked if he saw any signs of this, he replied, "Yes, at every little mountain pass there was a fort with wire entanglements. The military was in evidence everywhere, in cities, villages, the countryside, all."

Edison would never return to Paris. He spent the remaining two decades of his life in America, admired as a national hero. His genius had given the world light bulbs, phonographs, and the marvels of moving pictures.

The Return of Eiffel

Years after the Panama Canal scandal and Eiffel's brief time in prison, the once-famous engineer found himself living well. His home in Paris was a splendid mansion in a fashionable neighborhood. It was fitted with antique furnishings, crystal chandeliers, and Oriental rugs.

Upstairs in his study, Eiffel sat behind a huge

wooden desk with many secret drawers. There
he tended to business affairs or wrote scientific
papers. He had also started writing parts of what
would become an account of his life.

Never idle, Eiffel now had the time to devote
to studying a subject that had fascinated him for
a long time: the weather. When the Eiffel Tower
opened, he had installed a weather station to
monitor temperature, humidity, wind speed and
direction, rainfall, and weather conditions in
general. Later he would set up another twenty-
five such stations across France, paying for them
all himself. Starting in 1903, he published, again
at his own expense, a series of weather atlases.

Above all, Eiffel studied wind. As an engineer
of large structures, he had come to regard wind
as "an enemy against which I had to struggle
constantly." He was interested in the effects of
wind on aviation, or flight. He wanted to know
which shapes moved most easily through air. On
many days, Eiffel could be seen, his beard now
gray and white, at the foot of the Eiffel Tower. He
watched and calculated as objects came hurtling
down a wire that hung from his lab high in the
tower. By 1905 he had dropped hundreds of
objects from the tower.

For a long time, Eiffel had owned a residence in the French countryside. Soon after his disgrace, however, he seemed to take pleasure in collecting luxurious properties in other parts of France. Like newspaperman James Gordon Bennett Jr., he kept a steam-powered yacht in a harbor on the French Riviera.

In these years, Eiffel became a grandfather. He enjoyed the role, gathering his offspring for holidays at his various estates. He taught his young grandchildren how to swim and fence, activities he had always enjoyed. Eiffel's birthday each year was a grand, formal event featuring famous singers and musicians.

But what concerned Eiffel most in the period after the 1889 Paris world's fair was the fate of his beloved tower.

The Fate of the Tower

Another world's fair took place in Paris in 1900, eleven years after the Eiffel Tower opened. The tower was a major attraction at the 1900 fair, but it was not the centerpiece, as it had been in 1889. Eiffel's twenty-year contract would end in 1909, and those who had never liked the tower happily looked forward to it being taken down in that year.

The public's love for the tower had cooled. In 1900, only a million sightseers went up the tower, half as many as in 1889. Between fairs, the tower attracted about two hundred thousand visitors a year. But Eiffel had intended his tower to be more than a sightseeing attraction.

From the start, Eiffel had worked to show that the tower was a vital aid to scientific study. Now even those who had scoffed at the tower from the start admitted that it had proven its value to science. Eiffel had also said from the start that the tower had military uses. As early as 1888, while he was building the tower, Eiffel had realized that his monument might be saved by the new technology of radio and wireless telegraphy (sending signals through the air). He invited a French radio pioneer to experiment with a radio transmitter on top of the tower. Yet it was not until 1903 that Eiffel could persuade the French military command to put an officer with a telegraphy unit on the tower—and it was done then only because Eiffel paid for it.

Meanwhile, Paris officials had set up a committee to give advice on tearing down the tower. Just as the military officer took up his telegraphy post on the Eiffel Tower, the committee argued fiercely about whether to remove the tower. It concluded that some people still considered the tower an eyesore, but that it had value to weather science, aviation, and telegraphy.

The committee also wondered how people in other countries would react if Paris tore down the tower. This concern was summed up in a question: "Do you not think that the world would be astonished to see us destroy something in our city which continues to be a subject of astonishment for others?" So the city of Paris remained undecided about the future of its controversial landmark.

In the spring of 1906, Eiffel rejoiced to learn that his beloved tower would receive a new lease on life. The city of Paris extended his contract to 1915. The committee showed no great enthusiasm, however. It stated, "If [the Eiffel Tower] did not exist, one would probably not contemplate building it here, or even perhaps anywhere else; but it does exist." The official attitude was "Since it is there, let it stay"—at least until 1915.

Energized by this victory, Eiffel expanded his research in wind and aviation. He built a large wind tunnel at the foot of the tower and used the tower's electrical generators to power fans. They blew a steady wind of up to forty miles an hour. This let Eiffel conduct thousands of experiments that helped bring about the redesign of airplane wings and propellers. His book *The Resistance of the Air and Aviation* won an award from America's Smithsonian Institution in 1913.

By then, Eiffel no longer worried about the future of his tower. In 1908 the French War Department had come around to his point of view. It declared that a wireless telegraphy instrument in the Eiffel Tower "would prove most useful as a part of the national defense in time of war."

The Newspaperman and the War

James Gordon Bennett Jr. had started the Paris *Herald* as an English-language paper for the hordes of Americans who were expected to come to Paris for the 1889 fair. Once the flood of Americans had gone, he kept the paper going. It lost $100,000 a year, but Bennett could afford it. At that time, his original paper, the *New York Herald*, made $1 million a year.

As a boss, Bennett was unpredictable and sometimes terrifying. The staff of the Paris paper bribed his butler to let them know whenever Bennett left his apartment angrily, heading toward the office. He was equally unpredictable at home. One story often told about his behavior is that he was standing in front of his fireplace, struggling to get something out of one of his pockets. He pulled out a large roll of money. It wasn't what he was looking for, so he flung it in irritation into the crackling flames. A guest rescued the large sum of money, waited while Bennett got what he wanted from his pocket, and then handed the money back to his host.

"Perhaps that is where I wanted the roll," Bennett said, and threw the money back into the fire.

The horseless carriage (or, as it soon came to be called, the automobile) was making news in the early years of the twentieth century. Bennett's Paris paper covered this and other new machines in breathless detail, with lavish pictures. He also loved the new automobile races that sent fast machines careening across the French countryside. He could not resist sponsoring such a race, which he named after himself.

In early August 1914, war came to Europe, as many had feared. It was the start of the conflict

View of Paris from
the arched balcony of
the Eiffel Tower, Paris
Exposition, 1889.

THE TOWER IN WARTIME

GUSTAVE EIFFEL HAD LONG ARGUED THAT HIS thousand-foot tower would have value in a time of war. During the early weeks of World War I, he was proven right.

The war broke out in August 1914. That same month, the radio receiver on the tower captured a message from a Prussian commander named General Georg von der Marwitz. His division of mounted soldiers was bearing down on Paris. The message revealed that he was stuck—he had run out of food for the horses and couldn't advance. This piece of information, snatched from the air by the Eiffel Tower, helped convince the French military commanders to launch a counterattack against the Germans. That counterattack became the Battle of the Marne, the first big battle of the war, in which the French and their British allies won an early victory over the German invaders.

The radio station in the Eiffel Tower captured other enemy messages. Some of them led to the exposure of German spies, including the notorious female agent Margaretha MacLeod, known as Mata Hari.

now known as World War I (1914–18). On one
side were France, Great Britain, Russia, a few
other European countries, and eventually the
United States. On the other were Germany,
Austria-Hungary, Turkey, and Bulgaria.

Bennett's many automobiles, horses, and
carriages were taken by the French government
for the war effort, like those of everyone in
France. Bennett was seventy-three, but he had no
intention of abandoning Paris. He walked every
day to the offices of the Paris *Herald*, which
he turned into a lifeline of information for the
thousands of Americans who were stranded in
Europe by the chaos of war.

In the newsroom of the *Herald*, an editor
marked the position of the various armies with
pins on a map. When the armies came too close
to Paris, though, the editor fled. Not Bennett.
Most of his staff was gone by September, but he
took over as managing editor and also worked
as a reporter. As the war dragged on, many
Paris papers stopped publishing altogether.
Bennett started printing two front pages for the
Herald, one in English, as usual, and the other in
French, to give Parisians the news. He also used

his New York paper to urge the United States to enter the war against Germany.

The Paris *Herald* was losing more and more money, and by now Bennett could not easily afford to keep it running. The glory days of the *New York Herald* were past. It was still profitable, but it no longer made as much cash as before. Bennett was forced to economize. Among other changes, he sold his yacht to the Red Cross. In the fall of 1917 he visited wounded soldiers in a Paris hospital and caught the flu. He recovered, only to come down with pneumonia. He died in May 1918 at the age of seventy-seven. The great news story of his final years, World War I, was not over until months later.

The French newspapers genuinely mourned the death of this famous American. "It is a great pity, in all sincerity," one of them said. "And what a friend of France!"

The Test of Time

Peace finally came to war-weary Europe in late 1918. Gustave Eiffel watched with satisfaction as the public once again flocked to his famous tower. He was pleased that no person or nation had managed to build a structure that came close to being taller than his tower, and that the tower had proven its usefulness and value.

Eiffel finished writing the story of his life in 1923. Three months later, he died at the age of ninety-one. His tower was not surpassed in height until 1929, when the 1,046-foot Chrysler Building went up in New York City.

"I ought to be jealous of [my] tower," Eiffel once said, only half joking. "It is much more famous than I am." He was right. He is now largely forgotten, but his iron tower has become only more famous with the passing years. It may be the most instantly recognizable structure in the world. It is definitely the supreme symbol of Paris and French culture.

In 1889, when Eiffel first held court in his apartment in the sky, two million people visited the Eiffel Tower. One hundred and twenty years later, six million people a year waited in long lines for the pleasure of going up the tower. Mega-skyscrapers long ago overshadowed the Eiffel Tower in terms of height. But nothing else made by human hands has ever rivaled the tower's powerful mixture of elegance, size, and complexity when seen up close and in person. The tower comes to life as crowds clamber up and down its stairs and ride its elevators, and when they dine and eat and flirt on its platforms high in the sky. And visitors still feel that touch of unease when they gaze far below to see Paris spread out beneath them.

The Eiffel Tower still appeals to the human fascination with science and technology and to the human desire for pleasure and joy in life. In 1889 a French philosopher declared, "We are all citizens of the Eiffel Tower." Those words are as true today as they were then.

The Eiffel Tower in 1932, an iconic symbol of Paris.

347

Image Credits

4–5	Library of Congress (LC)
8	LC
14–16	LC
24	LC
30–32	LC
46–47	Otis Elevator Company
50–51	LC
55	Otis Elevator Company
60	Otis Elevator Company
62–63	LC
66	LC
75	Otis Elevator Company
77	Réunion des Musées Nationaux/ Art Resource, N.Y.
90–91	LC
92	Otis Elevator Company
97	Denver Public Library, Western History Collection, Z-330
100–101	LC
105	LC
109	Wikimedia
110	LC
132–133	LC
138	LC
144, top	LC
144	No source listed
147	Denver Public Library, Western History Collection, Nate Salsbury Collection, NS-321
149	Buffalo Bill Historical Center, Cody, Wyoming; 1.69.442
154–155	LC
157	Denver Public Library, Western History Collection, Nate Salsbury Collection, NS-328
161	No source listed
164–165	LC
169	LC
173	LC
175	Buffalo Bill Historical Center, Cody, Wyoming; 1.69.442
176	Denver Public Library, Western History Collection, Nate Salsbury Collection, NS-349
182–183	No source listed
188	Denver Public Library, Western History Collection, Z-2386
196–197	LC
201	LC
202	LC
206–207	LC
218	LC
222–223	LC
230–232	LC
234	The Darke County Historical Society, Inc.
237	Wikimedia
238	LC
248	Denver Public Library, Western History Collection, Nate Salsbury Collection, NS-195
250–251	LC
254	LC
258	Réunion des Musées Nationaux/ Art Resource, N.Y.
266–267	LC
270–271	LC
276	Denver Public Library, Western History Collection, Nate Salsbury Collection, NS-311
278	Denver Public Library, Western History Collection, Nate Salsbury Collection, NS-360
283	LC
286	Denver Public Library, Western History Collection, Nate Salsbury Collection, NS-361
289	Denver Public Library, Western History Collection, Nate Salsbury Collection, NS-13
292–293	No source listed
304	LC
306	LC
316–318	LC
321	Denver Public Library, Western History Collection, Nate Salsbury Collection, NS-136
327	LC
330–331	LC
333	LC
342–343	LC
346	Otis Elevator Company

Index

JILL JONNES, who holds a PhD in American history from Johns Hopkins University, is the author previously of *Eiffel's Tower*, *Conquering Gotham*, *Empires of Light*, and *South Bronx Rising*. Founder of the nonprofit Baltimore Tree Trust, she is leading the Baltimore City Forestry Board's new initiative, Baltimore's Flowering Tree Trails. As a staff member of the 2010 Presidential National Commission on the BP Deepwater Horizon Oil Spill and Offshore Drilling, she wrote the first chapter of the report *Deep Water: The Gulf Oil Disaster and the Future of Offshore Drilling*. In the fall of 2011, she was a scholar studying Trees as Green Infrastructure at the Woodrow Wilson International Center for Scholars in Washington, DC. Jonnes was also named a National Endowment for the Humanities scholar and has received several grants from the Ford Foundation. She lives in the Baltimore area.

REBECCA STEFOFF has devoted her career to writing nonfiction books for young readers. Her publications include histories, literary biographies, an encyclopedia of maps, and numerous books on science and environmental issues. She has also adapted a number of landmark works in history and science, including Howard Zinn's *A People's History of the United States*, Jared Diamond's *The Third Chimpanzee*, Charles C. Mann's bestselling *1493*, and Ronald Takaki's *A Different Mirror for Young People: A History of Mulitcultural America*.

1493 for Young People
FROM COLUMBUS'S VOYAGE
TO GLOBALIZATION
Charles C. Mann, adapted by **Rebecca Stefoff**
The previously untold story of early globalization
by means of trade, slavery, and conquest.

A Different Mirror for Young People
A HISTORY OF MULTICULTURAL AMERICA
Ronald Takaki, adapted by **Rebecca Stefoff**
Takaki's multicultural masterwork is "a brilliant
revisionist history of America that is likely to become a
classic of multicultural studies" (*Publishers Weekly*).

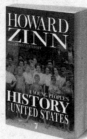

A Young People's History of the United States
Howard Zinn, adapted by **Rebecca Stefoff**
Zinn's modern classic brings to light the viewpoints of
those whose stories are rarely included in history books.

The Third Chimpanzee for Young People
ON THE EVOLUTION AND FUTURE
OF THE HUMAN ANIMAL
Jared Diamond, adapted by **Rebecca Stefoff**
Diamond's first foray into illustrated young adult
nonfiction is both an explosive indictment of human
nature and a hopeful presentation of the reasons
why the human species might well survive.

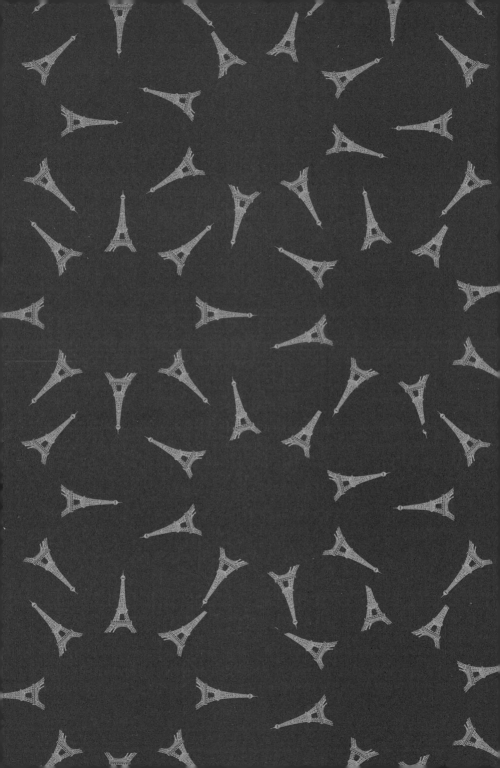